OPPENHEIMER'S ATOMIC BOMBERS

Russell Vandenbroucke

BROADWAY PLAY PUBLISHING INC
New York
www.broadwayplaypublishing.com
info@broadwayplaypublishing.com

OPPENHEIMER'S ATOMIC BOMBERS
© Copyright 2024 Russell Vandenbroucke

First edition: August 2024
I S B N: 979-8-88856-020-4

Book design: Marie Donovan
Page make-up: Adobe InDesign
Typeface: Palatino

The first version of OPPENHEIMER'S ATOMIC BOMBERS was produced as LOS ALAMOS REVISITED. It opened at the literary cabaret of the Mark Taper Forum (Gordon Davidson, Artistic Director; William P Wingate, Managing Director) on 15 April 1984. The cast and creative contributors were:

SCIENTIST .... Steve Peterman
WOMAN .... Elise Caitlin
MAN .... Bruce French

Director .... Robert Berlinger
Producer .... Russell Vandenbroucke
Associate Producer .... John Frank Levey
Production Coordinator .... Tom Schumacher

OPPENHEIMER'S ATOMIC BOMBERS was produced as ATOMIC BOMBERS as part of LA Theatre Works' "The Play's the Thing" (Susan Loewenberg, Producing Director) before a live audience and broadcast on KCRW to commemorate the 50th anniversary of Hiroshima, 6 August 1995. The cast and creative contributors were:

RICHARD FEYNMAN .... Jon Matthews
ARLINE GREENBAUM FEYNMAN .... Lisa Jane Persky
J ROBERT OPPENHEIMER .... Larry Cox
ENRICO FERMI .... Danny Mora
LAURA FERMI .... Jeannie Elias
LEO SZILARD .... Robin Gammell
ROBERT WILSON .... Tom Virtue
ARTHUR COMPTON .... Ron West
HANS BETHE .... Wolf Muser
WAC SECRETARY, WOMAN, VOICES .... Judy Scheer
VOICE .... Philip Mershon

Director .... Valerie Landsburg
Associate Producer .... Robert Robinson
Stage Manager & Foley Artist .... Amy Strong
Assistant Stage Manager .... David Spero

OPPENHEIMER'S ATOMIC BOMBERS opened as
ATOMIC BOMBERS at Northlight Theatre (Russell
Vandenbroucke, Artistic Director; Richard Friedman,
Managing Director) on 19 March 1997. The cast and
creative contributors were:

RICHARD FEYNMAN............................... Jeffrey Hutchinson
ARLINE GREENBAUM FEYNMAN..................... Debbie Bisno
J ROBERT OPPENHEIMER................................Karm Kerwell
ENRICO FERMI .... David Alan Novak
LAURA FERMI ....Lusia Strus
LEO SZILARD ....William J. Norris
ROBERT WILSON ....John Guzzardo
ARTHUR COMPTON.................................Glen Allen Pruett
GENERAL LESLIE GROVES..................................... Matt Penn
HANS BETHE ....Aaron H. Alpern
LEONA WOODS ....Maryke Huyding
various roles ....Kevin Kalinsky, Joe Gold, Bru Miller,
Jason G Wilson

Director ....Alan MacVey
Scenic & lighting design.................................John Culbert
Costume design... Nan Zabriskie
Dialect Director .... Nan Withers-Wilson
Recording Engineer ....Marty Higginbotham
Stage Manager .... Michelle A Kay
Dramaturgy Consultant...............................Susan V Booth

This play is informed by scores of books, articles, and reminiscences, but the author is especially indebted to Richard P Feynman for his permission to use stories from *Surely You're Joking, Mr Feynman* (New York: WW Norton, 1985).

CHARACTERS

RICHARD FEYNMAN, *1918-1988, native New Yorker (Queens), a wit in every sense of the word; tells his story in retrospect, but is in his mid-20s for most scenes; ranges from physics grad student to Nobel winner*

ENRICO FERMI, *1901-1954, Italian-born, dry, cool, and calm; physicist and Nobel winner*

J ROBERT OPPENHEIMER, *1904-1967, another native New Yorker, erudite and worldly; Scientific Director of the Los Alamos lab; physicist;*
also, SCIENTIST *helping with first chain reaction at Met Lab*

LEO SZILARD, *1898-1964, Hungarian, opinionated, strong-willed, politicized; physicist and inventor;*
also, LOCAL MAN *speculating on mysterious mesa activity*

ROBERT WILSON, *1914-2000, Wyoming-born, pious;* FEYNMAN*'s Princeton friend, slightly older but still his peer; physicist;*
also, SCIENTIST *helping with first chain reaction at Met Lab*

ARLINE GREENBAUM FEYNMAN, *1919-1945, New Yorker (Queens), tubercular,* FEYNMAN*'s match in wit; girlfriend then wife;*
also, VOICE *giving instructions at Trinity*

LAURA FERMI, *1907-1977, Italian-born, highly cultured; homemaker and writer;*
also, RAILROAD CLERK

ARTHUR COMPTON, *1892-1962, Midwestern minister's son; head of Metallurgical Lab (Met Lab) at University of Chicago; physicist;*
also, KLAUS FUCHS, *1911-1988, German-born émigré to England and* FEYNMAN's *friend; physicist*

GENERAL LESLIE GROVES, *1896-1970, rigid West Point graduate; head of Manhattan Engineering District;*
also, OFFICIAL VOICE-OVER *at Nobel ceremony*

HANS BETHE, *1906-2005, German-born, sensible, and down-to-earth as well as brilliant; physicist;*
also, LOCAL MAN *speculating on mesa activity*

LEONA WOODS, *1919-1986, member of* FERMI's *Chicago team; chemist;*
also, COED, TELEPHONE OPERATOR, LOCAL WOMAN *speculating, and as needed*

Also, SCIENTISTS, OFFICIALS, *and* CLERKS. *Two or three shleppers for physical activities are useful.*

Other doubling schemes are possible.

The use of actors should be as fluid as other production elements. Only FERMI *and* FEYNMAN *should not double. Historical anomalies of race and gender are welcome, but physics remains a game played by boys. These scientists were young:* OPPENHEIMER *was an elder who turned 40 at Los Alamos;* FEYNMAN *was 27 when the bomb dropped,* FERMI *all of 43. The bouillabaisse of accents reflects the diversity of the team of atomic bombers and reminds the audience how much the country depends on immigrants. The play can be performed with a cast of eleven: eight men, three women, but the support of three shleppers will aid any production.*

SETTING

Time: During World War Two (December 1938-September 1945), as conjured by the memories of Richard Feynman, *and his hindsight of the 1960s.*

Place: A stage; Stockholm concert hall; campuses of Columbia University, Princeton, and the University of Chicago; a Long Island hospital; a railway station; a secret lab in New Mexico and the surrounding high desert; an Albuquerque sanitarium.

PRODUCTION NOTES

Despite the (ultimately) grave subject of OPPENHEIMER'S ATOMIC BOMBERS, it should be approached playfully. After the war, Feynman fell into a slough of creative despondency and stagnation. He recovered his imagination and scientific creativity while watching a dinner plate thrown into the air of a Cornell University cafeteria and wondering about the relationship between the rate of spin at the plate's center and its wobble. He soon worked out the relatively simple equations to answer his question and then returned energetically to his work on quantum electrodynamics. He had temporarily lost his creative edge because he had lost his playfulness: "There was no importance to what I was doing, but ultimately there was. The diagrams and the whole business that I got the Nobel Prize for came from that piddling around with the wobbling plate." The play's humor is as essential as it is strategic: these men and women are surviving war; humor supports sanity in their daily lives. The demands of everyday life plus work that is deeply engaging easily distracts them from considering the purpose of life and the value of work.

ACT TWO's running time can be closer to ACT ONE's by cutting the speculation of Locals on page 62 and the Klaus Fuchs beat pages 64-66.

DESIGN

Choices should gracefully accommodate the fact that OPPENHEIMER'S ATOMIC BOMBERS has many transitions, both between scenes and within them. Scenes should move fluidly from one into the next as opposed to one stopping then the next starting. The characters are in a race; they cannot wait for scene changes. Blackouts are deadly. Use crossfades to avoid stop/start. Repositioning a blackboard on wheels facilitates many scene changes. Act and scene titles may be projected, a la Brecht. Productions should rely on sound, lighting, props, and costumes more than scenery.

Note on music: For performance of copyrighted songs, arrangements or recordings referenced in this play, permission of the copyright owner(s) must be obtained. Other songs, arrangements or recordings may be substituted provided permission from the copyright owner(s) of such songs, arrangements or recordings is obtained, or songs, arrangements or recordings in the public domain may be substituted.

The blackboard equations and explanations of "Numeracy" in ACT TWO were given to me by Freeman Dyson. Fermi's drawing of a boron bubble in that scene is from Robert Serber, *The Los Alamos Primer: The First Lectures on How To Build an Atomic Bomb* (Berkeley: University of California Press, 1992).

Special Thanks: Laurie Brown, Northwestern University; Rick Davis; Freeman Dyson, Institute for Advanced Study, Princeton University; Helen Merrill; Paul Owen; Michael Philippi; Justin Arthur Vandenbroucke, University of Wisconsin.

In memory of
Arthur Cyril Vandenbroucke, Sr
gentle man, hardware man

"By indirections find directions out"
Hamlet

ACT ONE:
Campus Cloisters

Prologue:
The Prize!

(In black, the strains of the fanfare of Mussorgsky's "Pictures at an Exhibition".)

VOICE OF OFFICIAL: To Professor Enrico Fermi of Rome for the discovery of new radioactive elements and for your discovery of nuclear reactions affected by slow neutrons. I ask you to receive the 1938 Nobel Prize.

(Lights up on FERMI, *formally dressed in a top hat and wearing a medal as he stands beneath a chandelier. Applause builds as he promenades down a red carpet, waving to the crowd comprised of the company of actors. Photographers fire away and his wife, modestly dressed and ready to travel, joins him.)*

FEYNMAN: *(Also formally dressed, appearing from the side, a suitcase and teddy bear in his hands. His voice, strongly accented by his native New York, stops all other stage action in a soft freeze. He speaks directly to the audience.)* Stockholm Concert Hall. December 10, 1938. Quite a day. Enrico Fermi was a scientist's scientist. Only a few years later I, little Ritchie Feynman, had the privilege of working beside this great man. He'd planned his escape from Europe ahead of time. After the ceremony, he and Laura, his wife, slipped away, sailed the

Atlantic, and waved to the Statue of Liberty in New York, my New York.

(FEYNMAN *hands the suitcase to* FERMI, *a teddy bear to* LAURA FERMI. FERMI *gives his top hat to* FEYNMAN. *The* FERMIS *wave goodbye and disappear in a final photoflash.*)

FEYNMAN: Like all immigrants, the Fermis had to take an aptitude test. They had to add 15 and 27, then divide 29 by 2. (*Mock surprise*) They passed. Enrico's slow neutrons had split uranium atoms, but he didn't know that then. Still, given his incredible body of work, he deserved the glittering prize. Not like some of the clowns they've picked.

(*Strains of the fanfare of Mussorgsky's "Pictures at an Exhibition" return, accompanied by the faint sound of live drumming as* FEYNMAN *riffs on his top hat. The crowd comes alive, refocusing on* FEYNMAN *as an official announces.*)

VOICE OF OFFICIAL: For quantum electrodynamics with deep consequences for the physics of elementary particles, I ask *you*, Professor Richard Feynman of Pasadena, California, to receive the 1965 Nobel Prize.

(FEYNMAN *dons the top hat jauntily and promenades down the red carpet. Applause builds until the photographers and their flashes stop him short. He listens to a hubbub of overlapping voices, "Over here", "Hey!" "Please, Professor Feynman, have you got just a minute, sir?"*)

FEYNMAN: Listen, buddy, if I could tell you in sixty seconds what I did to win, it wouldn't be worth the Nobel Prize.

(*The crowd laughs then departs, except for Wilson. With a nod,* FEYNMAN *invites the photographers to strike the carpet. He removes his coat and top hat then passes them to* WILSON. *These actions will be mirrored in the Epilogue. Lighting transitions:* FEYNMAN *takes us back as memories of the past supplant his narration of the present. Addressing the audience again:)*

FEYNMAN: I'm a curious character, okay, very curious. I was born not knowing and have only had a little time to change that here and there. On the way back from Stockholm, I visited my high school in Far Rockaway. I looked up my records, which was very interesting. My grades weren't as good as I remembered. That was disappointing. My IQ wasn't so great either, something like 124 or 126, but that delighted me. Winning the Nobel Prize was no big deal, but winning it with an IQ of only 124, that's something.

I'd been back to New York many times during World War Two and after. When it ended, I was the first Group Leader to leave Los Alamos and return to civilization. Sitting in a restaurant on 59th Street, I began to think, you know, about the radius of the Hiroshima bomb damage…. How far from here is 34th Street? The Empire State Building…all those apartments, businesses, all smashed. Later, when I saw people building a bridge, or making a new road, I thought they were crazy, they just don't understand. Why are they making new things? It's so useless. Fortunately, it's been useless for decades. So, I've been wrong for decades, and I'm glad those people had the sense to build bridges and roads, and so on.

You've heard Bob Seger's lyric, "Wish I didn't know now what I didn't know then"? Nice turn of phrase, but it's utterly impossible. There's no way we canNOT know what we know. Nuclear physics used to be an amateur game played by a few score professors and their grad students. Einstein was considered a mathematician for crying out loud. Nowadays, people call us what we are, if not worse. Society has experienced the power of physics.

I used to walk through incredible Los Alamos canyons and ancient Indian ruins with John von Neumann, the Hungarian mathematician I'd met at Princeton. He gave me an interesting idea: *(Von Neumann's accent)* "You don't have to be responsible for the entire world you're in". I developed a very powerful sense of social irresponsibility as a result, which has made me a very happy man. I'm indebted to Johnny for planting that seed. What do *I* care what other people think!

Most people who talk about working on the bomb, people in higher echelons, worried about big responsibilities. I worried about no big responsibilities. I was always flittering about underneath. I wasn't famous; I didn't even have my Ph.D. when I started. Later, I'd meet biggies like Compton, Oppenheimer, Einstein... *(Trailing off) But first,* imagine March 1939. Germany just annexed Czechoslovakia. I'm close to graduating at M.I.T, your ordinary undergraduate.

(A young woman sashays by. FEYNMAN establishes the Columbia lab by setting stool and blackboard in place. Formulas and drawings accumulate on it through the play as old marks remain while new ones are added.)

FEYNMAN: In New York, at Columbia University, Enrico Fermi confers with Leo Szilard, your ordinary geniuses.

(FEYNMAN snaps his fingers; they enter or come to life as he exits to find the coed.)

Scene One:
New-Found Land

(SZILARD: Hungarian accent, shabbily dressed compared to FERMI. Friction between them is common. SZILARD is assertive and direct while FERMI tends to be polite, quiet, controlled, cool.)

SZILARD: I know it's hard to leave Europe, Laura. The history, the culture, the food, but it's safer here for a Jew like you or me. You'll love New York.

LAURA: *(Italian accent)* Eventually, Professor Szilard.

SZILARD: Much sooner.

FERMI: *(Also accented. It diminishes through time, but never disappears.)* I tell Laura, we start American branch of the family.

LAURA: Eventually. Five years to naturalize. Five years as alien. Alienated too.

SZILARD: *(To* FERMI*)* Niels Bohr told you about the Berlin experiment?

FERMI: Fission.

SZILARD: Yes.

FERMI: It excites my curiosity.

SZILARD: It excites my concern. Fission means bombs.

FERMI: Don't jump so fast ahead, Leo.

SZILARD: The first step to creating anything is conceiving it.

FERMI: There is only a *remote* possibility that fission of uranium would emit neutrons.

SZILARD: How can you…

FERMI: If it does, then a chain reaction could occur.

SZILARD: Surely you see…

FERMI: If a chain reaction sustains, *then* it might be possible to construct a device that…

SZILARD: *(Cutting him off.)* You doubt a chain reaction can sustain?

FERMI: Not at all. In twenty-five to fifty years.

LAURA: Einstein says turning fission into useful energy "is like shooting birds in the dark—in a country where there are not so many birds".

SZILARD: He said that about useful energy?

LAURA: *Newsweek* magazine.

SZILARD: What he says about destructive energy?

FERMI: I haven't heard.

SZILARD: I patented chain reaction process five years ago.

FERMI: I heard.

SZILARD: I assigned patent to British Admiralty. You heard that? *(No answer)* To keep secret from Germans. We have to withhold discoveries. Ration conversation too.

LAURA: *(Grasping* SZILARD*'s hint, over her shoulder as she exits.)* I go.

SZILARD: No one should publish anything significant. That's part of my plan.

FERMI: I heard.

SZILARD: No public seminars or conferences.

FERMI: Censorship I don't like.

SZILARD: What's to like?

FERMI: Leave applications to business and engineers. Not our concern. Science is pure and simple: research is research, knowledge is knowledge.

SZILARD: Enrico, our Garden of Eden is on brink of war bigger than last. We must concern ourselves with everything. There's more than science.

FERMI: You sound like a humanist.

SZILARD: Is that an insult?

FERMI: We should never censor ourselves.

SZILARD: We must think ahead, think of future. If we don't, government will. You prefer lives controlled again?

(No response)

SZILARD: You think chain reactions feasible in a few decades instead of months.

FERMI: Probability too remote.

SZILARD: How remote?

FERMI: Ten per cent.

SZILARD: If I had pneumonia and doctor told me I had ten per cent chance to die, I would be very concerned. What if ten percent chance Germany destroying us?

FERMI: Nuts.

SZILARD: I think chain reaction can happen soon; you think not. Should we flip a coin? *(Beat)* Let Nazis decide who's right?

FERMI: *(Softening to* SZILARD*'s argument)* You think they'd put Heisenberg in charge?

SZILARD: Certainly. *(Beat)* What does Hitler plan to do in Czechoslovakia? Cruise the Danube? Tour Prague Castle? *(Beat)* Plunder Europe's richest uranium mines?

FERMI: Nuts.

(Lights crossfade to FEYNMAN *entering opposite with a suitcase, reading from a book.)*

FEYNMAN: "Two August 1939. Dear Mr President: Some recent work by E Fermi and L Szilard leads me to expect that the element uranium may be turned into a new and important source of energy.... It may become possible to set up a nuclear chain reaction in a large mass of uranium. This new phenomenon would also lead to the construction of bombs.... Yours very truly... *(Closing the book, toying with the audience to prompt them to proffer the right name, then with a German accent)* A. Einstein. Four weeks later, Germany invaded Poland. World War Two began. *(Putting down his suitcase to establish his Princeton dorm room. He can push on an easy chair.)* I was beginning graduate school at Princeton when President Roosevelt appointed a Uranium Committee to fund government's start in nuclear weaponry. *(Cash register sound)* Six thousand dollars. Money began trickling down to Princeton, Columbia. FDR set the bomb in motion, but as far as anyone knows, he had a sustained conversation about its political and international meaning with no one.

Scene Two:
College Scholarship

(Crossfade to a conversation in media res at Columbia lab.)

SZILARD: *(A lead pencil behind his ear, entering in conversation with* FERMI.*)* Then Adamson says…

FERMI: He's the colonel?

SZILARD: *(Nods.)* Colonel Adamson says, *(Imitating Adamson)* "Scientists don't understand war". He lectures us then concludes, "It generally takes two wars to develop new weapons. So you see, professors, weapons don't win wars. Morale does."

FERMI: I did not know that.

SZILARD: Wigner begins, *(Politely, in a high-pitched voice, Hungarian accent)* "That's very educational, Colonel. I was under the mistaken impression weapons were essential."

FERMI: Sounds like Eugene.

SZILARD: "Since you've taught us that they are not, will you testify in Congress against increased appropriations?"

(FERMI *laughs.*)

SZILARD: Colonel Adamson turns to me, "How much you need for pencils?" "Not pencils, Colonel, graphite. To moderate the neutrons. To make them more powerful." "You can have it", and out we go. The three Hungarian conspirators. Enrico, we begin! (*Turning his pencil into a cigar, puffing it in triumph. In his excitement, he drops the pencil.*)

FERMI: (*Picking it up*) What are these rubber ends?

SZILARD: Erasers.

FERMI: Why put them on pencils?

SZILARD: To fix mistakes.

FERMI: Italian pencils have no erasers.

(*Both* FERMI *and* SZILARD *gaze down the barrel of the pencil. Beat*)

FERMI: Graphite on its way?

SZILARD: One and a-half tons.

FERMI: Pure?

SZILARD: As my hands. (*Holding them up*)

FERMI: And source for neutrons?

SZILARD: Eldorado Radium Corporation.

FERMI: They gave you uranium oxide?

SZILARD: Loaned, Enrico. Five hundred pounds. But call it "tubealloy".

FERMI: (*Misplacing the emphasis*) "Tube a-loy"?

SZILARD: (*Correcting the emphasis*) Tube al-loy! The British code.

FERMI: (*Tasting the words*) "Tube alloy"? What should we call our work?

SZILARD: Hmmm… (*Circling the stage, thinking "hard". He starts, stops, thinks he has an idea, then rejects it, resumes circling. Thinking is difficult! Then an inspiration.*) How about the egg-boiling experiment?

(FERMI, *speechless under* SZILARD, *has nothing better to suggest.*)

SZILARD: We start uranium-graphite assembly now. What we should call it?

FERMI: Hmmm… (*Unconsciously, he mirrors* SZILARD's *circling above, but in precisely the opposite direction, then inspiration.*) How about pila. An exponential pila.

SZILARD: In English, Enrico.

FERMI: It *is* English, Leo. Pila! Heap! Bunch!

SZILARD: Pile, Enrico, pile! Your vocabulary grows quickly; your accent shrinks slowly.

Scene Three:
Princeton Tiger

(*Crossfade to* FEYNMAN *perched on his suitcase beside* ARLINE GREENBAUM *in his dorm chair.*)

ARLINE: (*Attractive, auburn hair, New York accent. Frail*) Why did this lady upset you?

FEYNMAN: She's a fool.

ARLINE: She's the Dean's wife.

FEYNMAN: A pompous fool.

ARLINE: Everyone needs a function in life. Hers is etiquette patrol.

FEYNMAN: (*He imitates her vocally and mimes pouring tea.*) "Would you like cream or lemon in your tea, Mr Feynman." "I'll have both, Mrs Eisenhart." (*Laughing, hee-hee-hee*) "Surely you're *joking*, Mr Feynman."

Pompous fools drive me up the wall. You can talk to ordinary fools, but a pompous fool, a dishonest fool, a putting-on-airs fool. *Those* I cannot stand!

ARLINE: What do *you* care what other people think?

FEYNMAN: Putsy, I don't care…when I'm concentrating. Like last week's seminar. Wheeler, my advisor, tells Wigner about our work, okay? He's supposed to. Wigner schedules us, then tells Russell…

ARLINE: Who's he?

FEYNMAN: Astrophysicist. Then Wigner tells von Neumann…

ARLINE: Him?

FEYNMAN: Mathematician. The greatest. Then Wigner says, "Professor Einstein is going to attend". *(Beat)* You know who he is, right?

ARLINE: 1921 Nobel.

FEYNMAN: Right!

ARLINE: I thought *he* was the greatest mathematician.

FEYNMAN: Physicist. *(Back to his story.)* The day before, I'm kinda nervous. That morning, I start sweating. My advisor says he'll take the hard problems. I'm expecting my first seminar to be worse than Sunday tea with Mrs Eisenhart, but soon as we start, a miracle occurs.

ARLINE: Pretty rare for an atheist.

FEYNMAN: I'm writing formulas, I'm focusing on physics, and my nerves…vanish. I'm a fish slipping down currents, a bird soaring through space. I'm in my element. All I'm conscious of is physics, the ideas.

ARLINE: Feel better?

FEYNMAN: Especially with you visiting for the dance. And you're feeling…

ARLINE: Like we're apart too much.

FEYNMAN: No, the lump on your neck?

ARLINE: It comes, it goes, like visiting you.

FEYNMAN: Arline…

ARLINE: It doesn't hurt. My uncle says to rub it with omega oil.

FEYNMAN: What does your doctor say?

ARLINE: (*Avoiding the question.*) When you finish grad school, you'll be the doctor.

(FEYNMAN *laughs. Hugs* ARLINE. *They start to dance, slow and close.*)

FEYNMAN: Bell Lab came through with an offer.

ARLINE: (*Hugging him tighter*) You'll be home this summer!

FEYNMAN: Frankford Arsenal made one too.

ARLINE: You'd consider an Army post in Philadelphia over a private lab in New York?

FEYNMAN: I'm thinking.

ARLINE: Think about me! Name one enticement of Frankford Arsenal that I can't match, theoretically of course.

FEYNMAN: Calculating Bessel functions. (*Answering her incomprehension.*) Improving gun turret engineering.

ARLINE: You'd prefer that to me?

FEYNMAN: Only to the extent I prefer peace to war.

(ARLINE *nods.* ARLINE *and* FEYNMAN *dance to something like "Our Love". He spins her offstage as lights crossfade.*)

Scene Four:
Industrial Columbia

(SZILARD *working at the Columbia blackboard.*)

FERMI: (*Offstage.*) Leo, Leo! (*Rushing in, brandishing a letter, excited*) Columbia gets contract!

SZILARD: How much?

FERMI: First government contract! (*Reading*) "To support uranium-carbon experiment in which a chain reaction would sustain itself."

SZILARD: How much?

(*Turning to the blackboard and its formulae,* FERMI *writes* 10^5.)

SZILARD: $100,000…

FERMI: (*Still reading*) "For metallic uranium and pure graphite for the intermediate experiment."

SZILARD: We get more material for egg boiling and pile!

FERMI: Yes. Columbia will be first to beat the Germans.

SZILARD: And the Italians.

FERMI: (*Smiling*)And the Berkeley cyclotron. (*Pulling another document from his pocket*) President supports us. (*Reading*) "Full effort toward making atomic bombs is essential to the safety of the nation and of the free world. If atomic bombs can be made, we must make them first."

(FERMI *remains elated,* SZILARD *reserved.*)

SZILARD: We must separate much more… (*Whispering*) uranium-235…from the "tubealloy". And we need more than minute quantities of… (*Whispering again*) plutonium…to reach a critical mass.

FERMI: (*Still referring to the letter*) Government wants theoretical studies at Chicago…

SZILARD: Yes.

FERMI: Electromagnetic separation out at Berkeley.

SZILARD: Of course.

FERMI: Engineering studies through Standard Oil…

SZILARD: Standard Oil?

FERMI: Diffusers through Chrysler…

SZILARD: Chrysler!

FERMI: Up in Hanford, du Pont will…

SZILARD: DuPont! No, no, no. This will not work.

FERMI: What????

SZILARD: I refuse work with businesses!

FERMI: They work against Nazis too.

SZILARD: I refuse to work hand in hand with moneychangers!

FERMI: Government decides, Leo. It's out of our hands.

SZILARD: How they expect us to work with war profiteers?

FERMI: Cooperatively.

SZILARD: *(He takes this in.)* Corporations aren't democratic. They're authoritative.

FERMI: Don't you mean authoritarian, Leo?

SZILARD: Maybe.

FERMI: Your pronunciation good, Leo, but your vocabulary needs work.

SZILARD: Companies grab control…

FERMI: We must think ahead.

SZILARD: Anything to make a profit…

FERMI: Consider the practical applications…

SZILARD: Act as if they know exactly…

FERMI: There's more than science, pure and simple.

SZILARD: This is an outrage.

FERMI: *(Shouting)* Leo!!! *(Silence)* Czechoslovakia invaded, Monrovia occupied, Slovakia "protected," your Hungary in ashes.

SZILARD: What should I make with du Pont? Nylon stockings?

FERMI: No, Leo. Plutonium.

SZILARD: Pluto: God of the underworld.

FERMI: God of wealth.

SZILARD: God of the dead.

(Beneath the strains of something like "Sing, Sing, Sing," an assistant begins slow procession upstage carrying a container that is heavy and messy. He chants "graph-ite" as he moves toward the Columbia lab, then offstage as if to deliver his load. A second shlepper, slightly smaller and weaker than the first, begins to cross the stage carrying a similar load with a similar chant. Finally, a third shlepper smaller and weaker still does the same. All three wear goggles and lab coats that grow dirtier by the end of the act. FERMI and SZILARD watch them as lights crossfade.)

Scene Five:
Princeton Industry

FEYNMAN: *(Also listening to "Sing, Sing, Sing")* "These principles, at first sight at such variance with elementary notions of causality, do in fact suggest, imply…lead…"

(Lost in dissertating, FEYNMAN drums a pencil in complex rhythms on his desktop. Stops, writes a sentence or two, drums again, this time with two hands to something like Gene Krupa solo in "Sing, Sing, Sing".)

WILSON: *(Rushing in)* They want to fund my idea.

FEYNMAN: Who's "they".

WILSON: I'm not supposed to say "who".

FEYNMAN: Okay. What's your idea?

WILSON: I'm not supposed to say "what".

FEYNMAN: Why do "they" want to fund "it"?

WILSON: I'm not supposed to say "why".

FEYNMAN: How come, Bob?

WILSON: I'm not supposed to say "how".

(FEYNMAN raises his hand, palm open, mouths the word "how" as in a Hollywood Western. WILSON doesn't follow.)

FEYNMAN: What are you talking about?

WILSON: It's a secret.

(FEYNMAN returns to dissertation.)

WILSON: I'm not supposed to tell anyone, but…

(Simultaneously:)

WILSON:	FEYNMAN:
I have to tell somebody!	You have to tell somebody!

FEYNMAN: Why me?

WILSON: I need you. Soon as you know what's going on, you'll have to join us.

FEYNMAN: To do what, precisely?

WILSON: *(Taking a deep breath)* Theoretically, there are two ways to create a chain reaction, right? They're trying one at Columbia.

FEYNMAN: The Pope's in charge.

(Responding to WILSON's quizzical look:)

FEYNMAN: Fermi…Italian…infallible.

WILSON: *(Takes this in)* Here's my idea. Instead of slowing down neutrons so U-235 captures them like Fermi's doing, we separate U-235 from U-238 using my isotron. Enough 235 might constitute a critical mass…

FEYNMAN & WILSON: *(Simultaneously)* to make a bomb.

WILSON: *(Surprised)* You know?

(FEYNMAN *shrugs.*)

WILSON: If it can be done, we should do it first. Not the Germans and Heisenberg.

FEYNMAN: "They" want to develop your idea?

WILSON: They're recruiting at Chicago, Berkeley, MIT, Illinois, here. You oughta come to the meeting.

FEYNMAN: I don't want to.

WILSON: Seaborg says: "No matter what you do the rest of your life, nothing will be as important to the future of the world as your work on this project". War has come to campus without being declared.

FEYNMAN: I don't want to. I'm writing my dissertation. I had lots of war work in Philadelphia last summer. And my sweet girl is in the hospital.

WILSON: What do they say this time?

FEYNMAN: "Say", indeed. Doctors never "know". They have no business calling themselves scientists.

WILSON: They ruled out typhoid?

FEYNMAN: *(Nods)* They're looking at Hodgkin's then lymphoma or lymphosarcoma.

WILSON: Lord have mercy. What are you gonna do?

FEYNMAN: Get married.

WILSON: Congratulations! Arline's a wonderful girl.

FEYNMAN: I think so, but my mother's beside herself.

WILSON: Jeepers.

FEYNMAN: "You have no idea what hardships lie ahead." Blah, blah, blah.

WILSON: Mothers! I can't believe someone younger than me getting hitched.

FEYNMAN: Did I tell you my marriage invention? I've noticed that two intelligent people, clearly in love, sometimes end up angry and fighting once they marry.

WILSON: Very perceptive.

FEYNMAN: If Arline and I disagree intensely, we'll discuss the matter later, okay. Within an hour reason will win out. Therefore, no more argument. QED.

WILSON: And when you can't resolve the differences in an hour?

FEYNMAN: (*Smug. He's thought of this too.*) We calmly, logically, agree to let one of us decide.

WILSON: Who?

FEYNMAN: It should be the older and more experienced one.

(WILSON *looks puzzled.*)

FEYNMAN: That would be me.

WILSON: You're talking about Arline *Greenbaum*? You'd make more sense tagging along with me.

FEYNMAN: No, I'm *trying* to write my dissertation. .

WILSON: Okay, but it starts at three. See you there.

(WILSON *exits as* FEYNMAN *calls after him:*)

FEYNMAN: Bob. Bob! It's all right that you told me the secret because I'm not going to tell anybody… (*Yelling down hall, then to himself*) but I'm not going to do it. (*Returns to his dissertation*) "These principles…" (*He begins to drum, rises, checks his watch, decides.*) Oh hell, wait up! (*Jump cut, directly to the audience*) By four o'clock I was calculating the total current you get in an ion beam, and so on. *(Conspiratorial, intimate with the audience)* Ion beam? I'll save you the details, trust me. I was working as hard and fast as I could so the fellows building the apparatus to separate uranium isotopes could do it at Princeton, okay?

The boys decided to work on this and stop their research. Science stopped during the war except the little bit done at Los Alamos. And that was mostly engineering.

(As lights begin to shift, a tremendous series of explosions.)

FEYNMAN: Pearl Harbor. A day that *still* lives in infamy.

Scene Six:
Chicago Blues

(Crossfade to the FERMIS *in their darkened basement. They whisper furtively as he reads a telegram with a flashlight.)*

FERMI: "Dear Professor. Stop. We need your help. Stop. Arrive Wednesday to consolidate in Chicago. Stop. Arthur Compton."

LAURA: Why Columbia can't be center?

FERMI: We tried.

LAURA: Not hard enough.

FERMI: Leo told Compton how hard moving forty tons of graphite is.

LAURA: Good for Leo!

FERMI: High ups say work should be… *(Not sure of the English word, he gestures with his hands apart then coming together, the opposite of* OPPENHEIMER*'s gesture below with* COMPTON *to denote "bomb".)* …centralizzato?

LAURA: Centralized?

FERMI: Centralized! during war. Everyone wants his own place. One praises Princeton, we want Columbia, Compton argues, "At Chicago we'll finish by year's end". He wins.

LAURA: *(Her voice rising)* Chicago is Wild West, Al Capone.

FERMI: Shhhh! Chicago is *mid*-west. Central, easy travel, many trains *(Hands together again)* meet. Leo going also.

LAURA: Enrico, first our homeland at war. Now, new home same. American neighbors battle Italian cousins. Passing newsstands on way to school, Giulio asks, "Are we fascists, Mommy?" Nella taunted as enemy alien. Enrico, please, we need safe. We need secure. New York supposed to be permanent home. You promised, no?

FERMI: Last move, Laura. For science. If experiment proves theory, US must be first. We stay at Chicago then return to New York. How long can war last?

LAURA: Thirty years!

FERMI: Laura…

LAURA: *(Conceding the argument)* Or until all West Coast physicists move East, and all East move west.

FERMI: *(Smiles wanly, hugs her)* No one can know where I go or why. Say lecture tour. You reach me through the Chicago's Met Lab.

LAURA: Metropolitan Lab?

FERMI: Metallurgical.

LAURA: They turn Nobel scientist into engineer?

FERMI: Depends on metal.

LAURA: *(Sighs with resignation)* Find us a nice Chicago apartment, caro. *(Retrieves their hidden cache)*

FERMI: Of course.

LAURA: After Giulio and Nella finish school in June, we join you.

FERMI: Certainly.

LAURA: Take the money.

FERMI: Not emergency fund.

LAURA: Yes, no one must freeze *these* enemy assets. *(She presents the lead pipe she'd retrieved from its hiding place within a coal bin. With sooty hands, she removes the wad of bills inside.)* From Alfred Nobel's hands and guilty conscience to yours.

FERMI: Dynamite.

(FERMI's hands become sooty in the money exchange. FERMI and LAURA kiss deeply.)

Scene Seven:
College All Stars

(Crossfade to shleppers burdened as before, moving downstage rather than crossstage since they have now relocated from New York to Chicago. The blackboard relocates too. Shleppers again enter one by one, this time to the drum-roll of a football fight song like "Bear Down, Chicago Bears". They are dirtier than before and continue their procession beneath the following introductions.)

(Once shleppers establish, FEYNMAN marches in wearing a shakos [drum major's hat]. His baton is a giant slide rule. He tweets a whistle from his lanyard as needed. Each teammate he introduces wears an identifying jersey or bib with a name on the back. On its front is a large symbol and smaller atomic weight of the chemical element evoking their specialty or identity. Once characters introduce themselves, with foreign accents when appropriate, he or she returns to the end of the line to assume a new persona. The lineup must be organized so GROVES, BETHE, COMPTON, and

OPPENHEIMER, *like* FERMI *and* SZILARD, *assume their parts when introduced. Litany sections like this should be rapid-fire.)*

FEYNMAN: The University of Chicago. Metallurgical Lab.

ANDERSON: *(Identified with Columbium, 41 Cb)* Herbert L Anderson.

FEYNMAN: Columbia University.

GROVES: *(76 Os)* Brigadier General Leslie R. Groves.

FEYNMAN: West Point.

WHEELER: *(61 Pm)* John A Wheeler.

FEYNMAN: My dissertation advisor.

SERBER: *(34 Se. Slight lisp)* Robert Serber.

FEYNMAN: University of Illinois.

ZINN: *(30 Zn)* Walter Zinn.

FEYNMAN: Canadian.

BREIT: *(101 Md. Looking none too happy)* Grigory Breit.

FEYNMAN: Russian.

TELLER: *(1 H)* Edward Teller.

FEYNMAN: Hungarian.

SZILARD: *(88 Ra)* Leo Szilard.

FEYNMAN: Still Hungarian.

FRANCK: James Franck.

FEYNMAN: *(32 Ge)* German. Nobel, 1925.

UREY: Harold Urey.

FEYNMAN: *(32 C)* Columbia. Nobel, 1934.

FERMI: *(100 Fe)* Enrico Fermi.

FEYNMAN: Nobel, Nineteen… *(Searching for the bright-eyed audience member who knows the answer)* …thirty-eight. That's right!

LAWRENCE: *(103 Lw)* Ernest O Lawrence.

FEYNMAN: Berkeley. Nobel, 1939.

SEABORG: *(94 Pu)* Glenn Seaborg.

FEYNMAN: Berkeley again. Co-discoverer of plutonium. Nobel, 1951.

BLOCH: *(97 Bk)* Felix Bloch.

FEYNMAN: Swiss. Nobel, 1952.

SEGRÈ: Emilio Segrè.

FEYNMAN: *(34 Se)* Italian. Fermi's oldest friend. Nobel, 1959.

WIGNER: *(71 W)* Eugene Wigner.

FEYNMAN: Hungarian. Nobel, 1963.

BETHE: *(2 He)* Hans Bethe.

FEYNMAN: German. Nobel, 1967.

(FEYNMAN removes hat and baton, which he passes to BETHE.)

COMPTON: *(Next to last of the remaining scientists.)* Arthur H. Compton.

FEYNMAN: Chicago. Nobel, 1927.

OPPENHEIMER: *(Finally.)* J. Robert Oppenheimer.

FEYNMAN: *(Aside)* Ethical Culture School—my mom went there! —Harvard, Göttingen, and Berkeley. She didn't go there. And I didn't get to go to Chicago, okay.

(The scientists—except COMPTON, OPPENHEIMER, and FEYNMAN—break from an upstage huddle they had formed after their introductions with a chant, "Fight! Fight! Fight!" and exit.)

COMPTON: You sounded perturbed.

OPPENHEIMER: The man in charge should know, Arthur.

COMPTON: Know what, Oppie?

OPPENHEIMER: A new possibility, a device powered by fusion.

COMPTON: Fusion of what?

OPPENHEIMER: Deuterium nuclei.

COMPTON: A hydrogen bomb. *(Beat)* I never thought of that.

OPPENHEIMER: Me either. Its mass can be anything; its potential is…

OPPENHEIMER & COMPTON: *(Grasping the concept)* Limitless.

OPPENHEIMER: Teller calls it "Super," concludes we should focus entirely on it. He won't work on anything else.

COMPTON: If we've thought of it, so has Heisenberg.

FEYNMAN: German, Nobel, 1932, Leipzig University and Kaiser Wilhelm Institute for Physics. Working for Hitler. *(Sits in his Princeton chair, loses hat and whistle)*

OPPENHEIMER: If it can be done, we should do it first.

COMPTON: What are the numbers?

OPPENHEIMER: Initial ones: five hundred times more powerful than fission.

COMPTON: *(Taking this in)* How do you create enough heat to burn the hydrogen?

OPPENHEIMER: A fission… *(Making a bomb gesture with his hands separating)* at the center of the super. *(Same gesture but bigger)*

COMPTON: Assuming we can make a fission…
(*Mimicking* OPPENHEIMER'*s gesture*).

OPPENHEIMER: Assuming. Teller got us thinking: If
it's hot enough to explode deuterium, would it be
hot enough to explode hydrogen in a nearby pond or
stream? A chain of lakes? The nearest ocean?

COMPTON: God in heaven above.

OPPENHEIMER: Nitrogen isn't much more stable.

COMPTON: (*Taking this possibility in*) No…

OPPENHEIMER: So, it might set the atmosphere on fire
too.

COMPTON: (*After a silence*) We'd be better off ruled by
Nazis.

Scene Eight:
Love Letters

(*Crossfade to* FEYNMAN *at Princeton opening an envelope
and* ARLINE *in her Long Island hospital bed. The author of
each letter speaks the words as the recipient reads them.*)

ARLINE: Dearest: It's not Hodgkin's, lymphoma,
or lymphosarcoma. Care to guess what? (*Beat*)
Tuberculosis. At least I can pronounce it. Your mother
is more distraught than ever—whether with me for
having this disease, or me for loving you, or you for
loving me, I couldn't say. I miss you terribly. What
does our future hold, Coach? What's in a name:
professor, fiancé, tuberculosis?

FEYNMAN: Pretty one: I'm relieved to know the truth,
aren't you? As I understand it, we're lucky: TB acts
more slowly than the others, and its outcome is less
certain. We have more time now so we can stop
rushing.

ARLINE: Richard—if "we can stop rushing," does that mean we're not getting married? That would make your mother the happiest woman on Long Island, but it could kill me. Please reply soon. I know you hate to write, but for me???

FEYNMAN: Putsy: You're silly when you're irrational. I asked you to marry me a long time ago and want to now as much as ever, but I can finish down here, then you can marry a doctor just like your parents planned the day their princess was born. My mother is…my mother. She writes like I'm away at camp. Be amused, like me, by my favorite parts:

ARLINE: "Arline should be satisfied with the status of 'engagement' instead of 'marriage', because in such a marriage you are not getting any of marriage's pleasures, only the severe burden."

FEYNMAN: "I am surprised the marriage you contemplate is not unlawful. It ought to be."

ARLINE: "Since I doubt you sincerely want to marry Arline, I think you are trying to please her just as you used to eat spinach to please me."

FEYNMAN: I never ate spinach to please her. I ate it to avoid her ire, which is different. See you for graduation. PS: Unlike spinach, I like the taste of you.

(FEYNMAN, *addressing the audience as he crosses to* ARLINE, *Mendelssohn's wedding march fades up:*)

FEYNMAN: After receiving my PhD, I borrowed a friend's station wagon, put some mattresses in the back, and prepared my Putsy for our honeymoon cruise.

(*A beaming* ARLINE *wears a wedding veil.*)

FEYNMAN: We slipped away from Long Island, sailed the Staten Island ferry past the Statue of Liberty in New York, my New York…

(A*RLINE* and F*EYNMAN* *wave.*)

FEYNMAN: …and married. No family, no friends, no synagogue, but we were husband and wife!

(F*EYNMAN* *places a ring on* A*RLINE*'s *finger. After a kiss— decidedly chaste, on the cheek—he picks her up and carries her off-stage as she throws confetti into the air.*)

Scene Nine:
Fermi Courts

(*Crossfade to* C*OMPTON* *crossing the Chicago campus as autumn leaves fall.* F*ERMI* *rushes on to intercept him, brandishing damaged mail. Emotional like never before.*)

FERMI: Arthur! Mail tampering! I could have stayed in Roma for this. Is enough I learn silly secret names? Surrender camera and binoculars? Have F.B.I. block my short-wave radio? Nuts to them and everyone else.

COMPTON: Enrico, let me…

FERMI: No privacy for physicists, no privacy for Italians, no privacy for war workers! If trusted for Met Lab, why no trust with mail? No rain, no snow, no sleet, no hail—and still no mail.

COMPTON: Maybe General Groves can fix it.

FERMI: (*Brandishing a letter*) Maybe he *already* fix it: "Professor, do not walk by yourself in evening", and "Professor, do not drive without escort to Argonne Lab". He calls scientists "expensive crackpots". We call him (*Imitating his girth*) "expansive idiot". I leave New York to work for *Manhattan* Project?

COMPTON: Buck up, man.

FERMI: Oopsy, Manhattan *Engineering* District.

COMPTON: It's the pressure, building delays at Argonne, meetings…

FERMI: I like solo work. I control details to control results. I like to *do* physics not profess it.

COMPTON: As chairman of the "Tubealloy" Committee, you have to attend meetings, read reports, write others, offer sage advice, guide the neophytes, placate officials, spur everyone on. *(Beat)* The Argonne carpenters are calling a strike.

FERMI: And we behind schedule already.

COMPTON: Can you wait a few weeks to begin?

FERMI: Can war wait a few weeks to end?

COMPTON: What should we do?

FERMI: Build pile here.

COMPTON: On campus?

FERMI: Yes.

COMPTON: That's insane.

FERMI: Can be safe.

COMPTON: Administration said it would turn campus inside out to win the war, not upside down. What if the pile explodes?

FERMI: We build in incremental steps, remove control rods in even smaller ones.

COMPTON: Our wives live in Hyde Park! My brother told mom, "If Chicago blows up, Arthur's experiment was a big success".

FERMI: *(Nodding)* Segrè told Laura, "Don't be afraid of being widow. If Enrico blows up, you will too."

COMPTON: *(Still not convinced)* It's too close to the Loop. Think of all the other families.

FERMI: Of course. How many have sons in Europe, Africa, Pacific?

COMPTON: President Hutchins should decide.

FERMI: He understands neutrons?

COMPTON: Less than our wives but university protocol…

FERMI: I plan slow, *controlled* chain reaction, Arthur. Suicide squad on top of pile douses with cadmium-sulfate solutions in emergency.

COMPTON: Who'd you draft for that?

FERMI: Graduate students.

COMPTON: *(Antipathy weakening)* Where could you fit three hundred tons of graphite?

FERMI: Three hundred fifty. Plus, forty of uranium oxide and six of uranium metal. You secure help moving it? University footballers? Monsters of the Midway?

COMPTON: Hutchins abolished the team. Guess what he told students who believe academic excellence is compatible with athletic strength?

FERMI: Enroll at Northwestern?

COMPTON: "Nuts." *(Beat)* Where would you put the pile?

FERMI: Stagg Field.

COMPTON: The middle of campus?

FERMI: *Under* the stands, Arthur. Squash courts.

COMPTON: *(Gazing towards Stagg Field)* When could it be ready?

FERMI: Depends how soon President Hutchins okays.

COMPTON: And if I decide?

FERMI: You disprove my theory that handsomeness is inversely proportional to intelligence.

COMPTON: When would it be ready, Professor.

FERMI: One month, Professor.

COMPTON: By year's end?

FERMI: We work two shifts, day team and night team.

COMPTON: *(Long beat)* You're the coach, Enrico. Be sure none of the players gets injured. *(Starts to exit but stops)* None of the spectators either. It's critical.

FERMI: I hope it will be.

(COMPTON *and* FERMI *exit separately.*)

FEYNMAN: *(With new kind of energy)* The Princeton team grew to thirty. The isotron was supposed to vaporize and ionize chunks of uranium. Once the uranium gave up an electron, it became electrically charged, and as it began to move through a magnetic field, the 235 and 238 would accelerate differently, and then… *(Studying audience)* anyone following this? Anyone interested in the details? Let's just say it was…complicated. Then it shut down. Berkeley's approach supported instead. Bob and Princeton physics took it hard. Nothing to do. *(Without a project, he becomes listless. Drumming, pencil tapping, and physical movements become legato. He's playing the audience, conspiring with it.)* Then we heard rumors of a secret lab for secret work in a secret place. *(He puts a finger to his lips, utters "shhhhhh," and tiptoes off the stage.)*

Scene Ten:
Beautiful Spacious Skies

(Music like Copeland's "Mexican Dance and Finale" from "Rodeo" crossfades to two men with binoculars studying the horizon above the audience.)

GROVES: You're sure this is the best place, Oppenheimer?

OPPENHEIMER: No, General Groves. That's why I brought you. It's your decision, after all.

GROVES: Damn straight!

OPPENHEIMER: With all your experience, I thought you'd make the best decision.

GROVES: Affirmative.

OPPENHEIMER: Still, there's a lot to recommend it.

GROVES: What's the biggest problem you foresee?

OPPENHEIMER: Relocating twenty-some homesteaders.

GROVES: Mexicans?

OPPENHEIMER: Mostly.

GROVES: *That's* your biggest problem?

OPPENHEIMER: And we'd have to displace the Los Alamos Ranch School, assuming it's willing to sell.

GROVES: Oppenheimer, it doesn't matter a good God damn what it's willing.

OPPENHEIMER: They've been here twenty-five years. Parents of the boys are plenty rich.

GROVES: So's government. It condemns what it wants, then grabs it for a price. Los Alamos has possibilities. It's secluded…

OPPENHEIMER: *(Cutting in)* Your guidelines emphasized that, General.

GROVES: For safety, Oppenheimer. I don't want folks busting their gums over "adverse effects" of "unforeseen results".

OPPENHEIMER: We're thirty-five miles from Santa Fe.

GROVES: What will the prima donnas think?

OPPENHEIMER: *(Puzzled)* There's no opera nearby.

GROVES: Your people, Oppenheimer. Scientists, longhairs, largest collection of eggheads ever assembled.

OPPENHEIMER: They know there's a war. The foreign ones have a personal stake. They've been closer to the front than me, General, or you.

GROVES: I didn't volunteer for this, Oppenheimer.

OPPENHEIMER: So, you've said, General.

GROVES: That Pentagon I built is the world's largest office building.

OPPENHEIMER: You've told me that too, General.

GROVES: When it opens, it will be ahead of schedule and…

OPPENHEIMER: *(Beating him to the punch line)* Under budget. So, you've said.

GROVES: Affirmative. We need to build an entire town. Roads, electricity, telephone lines, water…

OPPENHEIMER: *(Pointing)* The Rio Grande.

GROVES: *(Taking it in, then pointing)* And there?

OPPENHEIMER: Sangre de Cristo Mountains. *(Translating)* Blood of Christ.

GROVES: Uh-huh. *(Pointing another direction)* And there?

OPPENHEIMER: Bandelier National Monument. *(Explaining again)* Ancient ruins of Pueblo Indians. Cliff dwellings dating back a thousand years.

GROVES: How many workers you need now, Mr Scientific Director?

OPPENHEIMER: Two hundred… *(Afterthought)* …and fifty, including scientists and support personnel.

GROVES: You're sure?

OPPENHEIMER: Well…sure.

GROVES: First you said a nucleus of six scientists supported by technicians and services.

OPPENHEIMER: Yes, but then we…

GROVES: Then it was thirty scientists for three months.

OPPENHEIMER: Well, it's much clearer now that...

GROVES: Next, I heard a scientific staff of a hundred and...

OPPENHEIMER: Two hundred fifty should be enough.

GROVES: *(Beat)* Figure three hundred thousand dollars for construction. We need dormitories, offices, labs...

OPPENHEIMER: Classrooms...

GROVES: I thought they already had PhDs?

OPPENHEIMER: Some have children.

GROVES: Children!

OPPENHEIMER: Scientists put their slide rules up now and again.

GROVES: I hope the Chicago boys don't *ease* up their slide rules.

OPPENHEIMER: Enrico's working non-stop.

GROVES: That thing he's building better work.

OPPENHEIMER: It's an experiment, General, and theory has propounded that...

GROVES: Theory, shit! We need results. If it fails, we won't need a lab here or anywhere else.

OPPENHEIMER: I'm quite sure "the thing" will work, General.

GROVES: You seem so damn contented, Oppenheimer.

OPPENHEIMER: I spend summers on a ranch over there, but I never thought I'd combine the two things I love most.

GROVES: Namely...

OPPENHEIMER: Physics and the desert.

GROVES: New Mexico is beautiful country; I'll grant you that.

OPPENHEIMER: The Land of Enchantment. (*Crossfade*)

Scene Eleven:
For Every Action...

FEYNMAN: December 2, 1942. The Allies await a German counter-offensive in Africa. In the Pacific, marines battle on Guadalcanal. On the home front, gas rationing continues its second day. And in Chicago, the undefeated Bears are preparing for a rematch with the cross-town Cardinals. Down on the Midway, Enrico Fermi and his team are poised as well.

(FEYNMAN *exits as* FERMI *leads his team into the squash court. [*OPPENHEIMER *was not among them; the actor playing him can double here without* OPPENHEIMER's *distinctive hat.] They're wearing winter coats, hats, and gloves. Something like Steve Reich's "The Desert Music," Fifth Movement, plays beneath the scene and periodically builds to raise tension. One light bulb hangs from the ceiling. A telephone is affixed to a wall. The pile is off-stage, only its long control rods visible. The less seen the more believable. Scene light seems to emanate from the pile. The scientists huddle, as if in a football game, and evince the Chicago cold with their hands, feet, movement. When not specifically engaged in action or conversation, they are hypnotized by what is transpiring around them, their focus split between the pile and* FERMI. *He remains calm, in complete control. Tension derives from anyone but him. The pace of speech and action is slow, a counter to rising tension.*)

(*The experiment resumes with a voice from the middle of the huddle.*)

FERMI: Zip out safety rods on your side, rod. Herb, same on yours. George will handle the last one…

(Under the scene, two shleppers wearing goggles remove the rods extending through the entire pile. They are as long as possible; their manipulation evokes Chinese Opera. The shleppers become increasingly dirty from ferrying graphite bricks. Later, when they appear without goggles, their faces are smudged, their eyes in stark contrast like the mask of raccoons. After each rod is removed, a shift in music evokes increased clicks, ticks, whirs, and flutters of the offstage gauges. The third shlepper, George, is dressed the same as Wally and Herb. [Female names can replace as warranted by casting.] The huddled scientists separate until FERMI is revealed with his 6-inch slide rule, intent on his calculations. He repeats these throughout the experiment, marking numbers on slips of paper he holds dear. Throughout, he is the conductor of a great orchestra. His slide rule is his baton.)

COMPTON: I'm freezing.

FERMI: Rate should rise from 600 to 1200 per minute. *(A noise escalates.)*

COMPTON: *(Stomping his feet)* Just our luck, coldest day of the year.

SZILARD: You prefer egg soft-boiled?

FERMI: I'll give George orders on last rod.

SCIENTIST/LEONA WOODS: *(Referring to her clipboard and calculations.)* Look at its sensitivity to atmospheric pressure.

FERMI: Another layer of graphite bricks on top, Wally.

(FERMI calculates, is pleased with the results, as he is throughout the scene. Some scientists plot the exponential curve. Others refer to their notes, clipboards, and gauges. They glance at FERMI frequently.)

COMPTON: You trust him implicitly, don't you?

SCIENTIST/LEONA WOODS: He's the pope.

SZILARD: Enrico the First.

FERMI: Two more feet, George.

(Sounds intensify. A noise, loud as a thunderclap, raises tension to its highest level yet. Everyone is startled— jumping, shrieking, frozen in place—except FERMI, surprised at the response of others.)

SCIENTIST: Lord help me…

COMPTON: *(Overlapping.)* What the hell!

FERMI: Everything fine, Arthur. Neutron absorbing rod fell. Herb, move it to the other side. Now, zip out another foot.

(The sounds intensify.)

FERMI: More graphite bricks. Keep them coming until I say stop. Zip out one more foot, George.

(Noises and tension escalate.)

COMPTON: I can't stand this cold.

SCIENTIST/LEONA WOODS: Pretend you're in a warm climate.

SZILARD: North Africa, with a gun in your hand keeping you warm.

(COMPTON exits.)

FERMI: *(Pointing to a dial or gauge.)* It should level off right…here.

(It does, as communicated by sounds and music.)

FERMI: We're getting closer. More graphite and uranium oxide bricks, Wally.

(The noises rise. FERMI calculates.)

SCIENTIST/LEONA WOODS: When do we become scared, Professor?

FERMI: Never. *(He calculates.)*

(COMPTON *has retrieved a raccoon coat to ward off the cold.)*

FERMI: Take up hunting in the Argonne Forest, Arthur?

COMPTON: I found it in a football locker. Want me to get you one?

(But FERMI *is back to his calculations, gauges, and meters.)*

FERMI: *(Calling out.)* One more row of graphite bricks! At the 51st layer, the pile will be critical.

SCIENTIST: So calm…even for Enrico.

BETHE: So calm for anyone under such pressure.

FERMI: This should do it. The graph will rise without leveling out. Ready everyone? George, one more foot… now!

*(*FERMI *waits. Slow build to the loudest and most pleasing sound yet.)*

FERMI: The chain reaction has begun. The graph is exponential. The reaction is slow, self-sustaining, and controlled!

(How long can these moments of success sustain? FERMI'*s calm gives way to a broad smile. He closes his slide rule emphatically, returns it to his pocket. The response of others is utter stillness. The light bulb sways enough to pull focus. After what seems like an eternity,* FERMI *continues.)*

FERMI: Zip in! Lock rods in safety position. We return tomorrow morning.

*(*COMPTON *produces a bottle of Chianti from the folds of his coat. It and paper cups passed about. Only then does the tension of the day, the Manhattan Project, the war, explode in enormous cheers, shrieks, and cries.* FERMI *enjoys the collegial moment as much as a reclusive man can.)*

COMPTON: *(Raising his paper cup to toast.)* To Enrico Fermi, Salute!

SCIENTISTS: *(Many voices, languages, not in synch as if rehearsed.)* To Enrico, Salute! Ein Prosit! Cheers.

SCIENTIST: We were confident of your success.

FERMI: *Our* success. Let's hope we got here first—and that we get *there* first.

SCIENTIST: How much power did it produce, Professor.

FERMI: One watt. Enough energy to light up… *(Pointing)* one bulb.

COMPTON: *(He picks up the wall phone.)* Mary, get me Conant and the Committee. *(Back to* FERMI*)* Two weeks ahead of schedule, Enrico. They'll be surprised by the news. *(Into phone)* Jim? Arthur here. The Italian Navigator has just landed in the New World. The earth was not as large as he had estimated, and he arrived sooner than he had expected. *(Listens)* "Were the natives friendly?" *(Pause. He looks at the others grinning.)*

*(*SCIENTISTS *answer his question with loud cheers.)*

COMPTON: Everyone arrived safe and happy. *(Hangs up.)*

SZILARD: *(Breaking from the celebrants, he approaches* FERMI *as if to shake his hand.)* Enrico?

FERMI: Yes, Leo?

SZILARD: This will go down as a black day in the history of mankind.

SCIENTIST/LEONA WOODS: Professor, you have unlocked the door to the atomic age.

FERMI: For every answer there is at least one more question.

(The squash court door opens. A bright, inviting shaft of light flows in as "The Desert Music" resumes. The

SCIENTISTS *study one another uncertainly, then turn to*
FERMI *for guidance. He responds to the siren song of the*
future by leading the group on a serpentine procession.
They link hands like paper dolls, one-by-one, as an ever-
lengthening string of scientists follows FERMI *by latching on*
to the last scientist in line. Mimicking FERMI *in Follow the*
Leader fashion, they prance and dance sinuously throughout
the stage space of the lab, gradually gaining speed, and
heading to the light.)

FEYNMAN: *(Entering in time to observe some of this*
"dance") Chicago was no Second City that winter.
Especially to physicists. Through the door opened
here, everything important was heading west. Manifest
destiny. *(He hesitates before catching the hand at the end of*
the daisy chain. He pauses in the doorway, waves "goodbye"
to the audience, and is pulled into the blackout.)

END OF ACT ONE

ACT TWO:
Purple Mountain Majesties

Scene One:
Recruiting

(As intermission ends, before house to half, the audience hears something like Rudy Vallee singing unfamiliar lyrics about Einstein that precede the familiar melody of "As Time Goes By". After a few bars, a sharp telephone ring drowns out the melody. No physical phones needed)

FEMALE TELEPHONE OPERATOR: *(Unseen)* Long distance for Robert Wilson, please.

WILSON: *(Pinspot up on him, stage left)* Yes?

FEMALE TELEPHONE OPERATOR: Hold for J Robert Oppenheimer.

(WILSON squirms while waiting.)

OPPENHEIMER: *(Pinspot up on him, stage right)* Hi, Bob. How are you?

WILSON: Fine, Opie, why are you…

OPPENHEIMER: *(Cutting him off)* How's the recruiting going for…you know…

WILSON: Pretty well, sir. We've got everyone…

OPPENHEIMER: *(Cutting him off)* …that's great…

WILSON: …everyone but Dick.

OPPENHEIMER: Feynman? We must have him. I thought he stayed with your group.

WILSON: He did, but traveling so far out to…

OPPENHEIMER: He didn't seem like a mama's boy.

WILSON: No, you see…

OPPENHEIMER: …put him on the line.

WILSON: I'll get him. *(Exits)*

FEYNMAN: *(Entering after a beat)* Professor Oppenheimer?

OPPENHEIMER: Dick, what's this Bob tells me: You don't want to travel with the team?

FEYNMAN: Nothing like that, you see…

OPPENHEIMER: No, I don't see. Wasted time means wasted lives. I need you.

FEYNMAN: It's not me. It's my girl, my wife. She won't breathe so well out in…out there, high altitude. She's got TB.

OPPENHEIMER: Ah. *(Quickly strategizing)* Can you to give me a few days to work on this?

FEYNMAN: Sure, you think there's a way I could…

(Sound of click as OPPENHEIMER *ends call precipitously.* FEYNMAN *slumps as ACT ONE music of* OPPENHEIMER-GROVES *returns. Crossfade to* ARLINE, *dozing, sitting as she will be for the next scene, a blanket covering her legs and hiding her wheelchair.)*

*(*ARLINE, *awakening as* FEYNMAN *enters:)*

ARLINE: Dick? I was beginning to think my husband had forgotten me.

FEYNMAN: *(Entering jauntily)* Only in your imagination. *(Kisses her on the cheek. Sits beside her)*

ARLINE: Good day?

FEYNMAN: *Great* day! Oppie found a sanitarium. The altitude's lower so you'll breath better.

ARLINE: How close to your magic mountain?

FEYNMAN: He promised me time off to hitchhike down every weekend. Scout's honor.

ARLINE: *(Weighing possibilities)* This new job would help you become a professor?

FEYNMAN: Hope so. *(Brandishing)* Here's the orientation sheet they gave me.

ARLINE: Let's hear.

(Lights widen to reveal the FERMIS, *seated to mirror the* FEYNMANS. *The blackboard, in profile, might separate the couples. Their conversations interweave logically.)*

FERMI: They gave me an orientation sheet.

LAURA: Hmmpf. What it says about housing?

FERMI: "Two and four-family units…"

LAURA: *(Interjecting)* Tenements.

FEYNMAN: "Single rooms for bachelors and bachelorettes."

ARLINE: Bachelorettes?

FERMI: "Three, four, and six-room apartments for families."

ARLINE:	LAURA:
That's reassuring.	That's *not* reassuring.

ARLINE & LAURA: When would we go?

FEYNMAN:	FERMI:
Right away!	In a year or so?

ARLINE: A new adventure…

LAURA: We've had enough adventure.

ARLINE: Life outside New York for a change…

LAURA: I've lived too many places to change.

ARLINE: No kids to hold us back…

LAURA: Think about the kids.

ARLINE: Good for your career…

LAURA: Bad for *la famiglia.*

ARLINE: Let's go.

LAURA: Let's not go, Enrico, *ti prego.*

FERMI: *(Beat)* Not yet.

(FERMIS *exit.*)

ARLINE: I'm ready, pardner.

FEYNMAN: Giddy up.

Scene Two:
Trained Connections

*(Crossfade to something like "On the Trail" of Groffé's
"Grand Canyon Suite". SCIENTISTS enter separately, each
with a suitcase or briefcase. They begin out-of-synch pliés
as if riding horses. Some affect Western wear: boots, cowboy
hat, bandanna.)*

WILSON: *(Entering last, to his charges.)* Remember:
Princeton is a small station. It'll look suspicious if
everyone buys a ticket to New Mexico, okay?

SCIENTIST: Will do, buckaroo.

SCIENTIST: We fixin' ta hit the road lickety-split?

*(WILSON shrugs, unable to answer since he doesn't
understand the question. Music and pliés stop as a new lineup begins. Each actor is a different SCIENTIST. Each carries
his suitcase or briefcase. A clerk stamps their tickets, the
sound buttoning each request. FEYNMAN is in line with the
others.)*

SCIENTIST: One-way to Dallas please.

SCIENTIST: One-way to Denver, please.

SCIENTIST: One-way to Saint Louis, please.

FEYNMAN: With everyone buying tickets for somewhere else…

FERMI: *(On a different part of the stage, entering from an entirely different direction, carrying suitcase and tennis racket.)* Roundtrip to Knoxville, please. *(Exits)*

SCIENTIST: One-way to Kansas City, please.

FEYNMAN: I figured it wouldn't be suspicious if I just purchased… *(He approaches the clerk.)*

SCIENTIST: One way to Tulsa, please.

FEYNMAN: Two tickets to Albuquerque, please. One-way.

CLERK: Albuquerque?

FEYNMAN: Albuquerque.

CLERK: New Mexico?

FEYNMAN: New Mexico.

CLERK: *(Gesturing toward blackboard and unseen boxes offstage)* So, all this stuff is yours?

FEYNMAN: Christmas presents.

CLERK: In March?

FEYNMAN: *(Beat)* Passover?

CLERK: Un-huh.

FERMI: *(Reentering, now carrying hiking boots and suitcase)* Roundtrip to Yakima, please.

(Again, FERMI *exits while the others prepare for their trip. Something like "On the Atchison, Topeka, and Santa Fe" starts. The* SCIENTISTS *sit on their suitcases in rows*

suggesting a train. FEYNMAN *sits beside* ARLINE. *Sound of whistle as they lurch from the station.*)

(FEYNMAN *drums both to and against the sounds of steel wheels against steel rails.*)

ARLINE: (*Reading from a pamphlet.*) "The Los Alamos Ranch School is near the largest extinct volcano in the world… (*Paying closer attention*) where countless explosions blasted the earth's epicenter high into the prehistoric sky."

(ARLINE *and* FEYNMAN *exchange looks.*)

ARLINE: "Such a tumultuous past makes this an ideal place for geologists to unearth the secrets of nature."

(*Shared double take.* FEYNMAN *stops drumming.*)

ARLINE: "Adolescence is a crucial period. If a boy builds his health in the most safe and scientific manner, he is not likely to suffer breakdown later."

FEYNMAN: "Safe"?

ARLINE: "Scientific"?

FEYNMAN: "Breakdown"?

ARLINE: "The Los Alamos Ranch School is where boys become men."

(*Another train whistle, then sound of train stopping.* SCIENTISTS *exit, reassemble elsewhere for next scene as* FEYNMAN *rises and pushes* ARLINE *across the stage as if dancing with her. She's been in a wheelchair since intermission.*)

FEYNMAN: I'll be back next weekend.

ARLINE: Let's have steaks.

FEYNMAN: The doctors let you leave?

ARLINE: *At* the sanitarium. We'll barbecue on Route 66.

FEYNMAN: Surely you're joking, Mrs Feynman?

ARLINE: We'll pretend we're a normal married couple.

FEYNMAN: You expect me to barbecue while Albuquerque stares at us?

ARLINE: Dope, what do *you* care what other people think?

(ARLINE*'s got* FEYNMAN.)

FEYNMAN: I'll hitch back in a week. (*Starts to hug*) Kiss?

ARLINE: (*Gives him her cheek*) Someday I'll be better.

(*Shlepper as orderly wheels* ARLINE *away.* FEYNMAN *sticks out his thumb to hitchhike, and the blast of a truck horn meets him.*)

FEYNMAN: (*Ad-libs as he runs for his ride. Crossfade*)

Scene Three:
Conferring

(FEYNMAN *joins the assembling* SCIENTISTS *who are absorbing their gorgeous surroundings for the first time, mouths agape [figuratively].* OPPENHEIMER *moving the blackboard into place to denote the Los Alamos lab breaks their revery. The* SCIENTISTS *sit on their suitcases. Shleppers should now be in uniform as SEDs, members of the Army's Special Engineering Detachment.*)

OPPENHEIMER: Welcome to Shangri-la, gentlemen.

FEYNMAN: (*Furtively, to* WILSON) I thought we were supposed to call it Site Y?

OPPENHEIMER: I thought we should start with an introduction to review our progress and challenges ahead. Construction is a little behind,

(SCIENTISTS *react to* OPPENHEIMER*'s understatement.*)

OPPENHEIMER: but some equipment is on its way in boxcars.

FEYNMAN: What's ready to use?

OPPENHEIMER: *(With a piece of chalk in hand)* For theorists like us, Dick, there's this… *(Pointing to his head)* and this… *(Points to blackboard)* Let me intro…

(As OPPENHEIMER *turns to* GROVES, FERMI *arrives.)*

OPPENHEIMER: Enrico! Just in time.

FEYNMAN: *(To* WILSON*)* Bob! Look who's here.

OPPENHEIMER: Before the science, General Leslie Groves would like a few words.

GROVES: Welcome to Los Alamos, men. I want to impress how dependent we are on each other. Be vigilant every day, in every way, about what you say and who you say it to. For security, we're stringing the perimeter with barbed wire.

FEYNMAN: To keep strangers out or us in?

GROVES: Both. And because the work's so sensitive, I'm sure you'll understand why mail will be censored.

FERMI: You cannot censor civilians!

GROVES: Which is why you'll have to agree to it. You'll be restricted to the mesa, one visit to Santa Fe per month…

*(*FEYNMAN *stands to appeal to* OPPENHEIMER *but is mollified when he hears)*

GROVES: …unless special arrangements are made. We'll also use code. Physicists will be "fizzlers"; chemists are "stinkers". "Top" means "atom", and "topic" means… anyone?

WILSON: Atomic?

GROVES: Correct. "Boat" means "bomb", and "topic boat"…

SCIENTISTS: *(En masse, a class with no enthusiasm)* Atomic bomb?

GROVES: You boys are sharp. Plutonium is "copper", and uranium 235 is "magnesium" or "ten…"? Class?

(No response)

GROVES: "Ten…? Tenure!" Two plus three plus five equals ten, and "ure" is the first syllable of "uranium". "Ten-ure."

FEYNMAN: That oughta give Nazi codebreakers fits.

GROVES: Some of you get code names. Enrico Fermi?

FERMI: Present.

GROVES: You're Eugene Farmer. Arthur Compton?

OPPENHEIMER: He's in Chicago with Szilard.

GROVES: Which is precisely where Szilard's staying. Hans Bethe?

BETHE: *(Correcting the pronunciation)* Bethe.

GROVES: You're Hank Barker.

FEYNMAN: Hey, Groves!

GROVES: *General* Groves!

FEYNMAN: Is the Army planning to fool illiterates or the deaf and dumb?

GROVES: Who're you?

FEYNMAN: Bob Wilson.

WILSON: Dick!

FEYNMAN: Richard Feynman.

GROVES: *(Consulting his list)* Richard Feynman? *(Can't find his name)* You're so important, Feynman, we'll just call you…Dick. *(Beat)* That's it for today. *(Starts to exit, second thought)* You can start talking like fizzlers and stinkers. *(Laughs at his wit and exits)*

OPPENHEIMER: *(Reassuring his troops)* His bark's worse than his bite.

(Doubtful grunts, growls, barks)

OPPENHEIMER: I got him to change his mind about putting us in uniforms.

(Responses)

OPPENHEIMER: The military wanted information compartmentalized, to keep secrets from one another, but that would slow us down and make it less likely we'd get there first. We need to share ideas, theories, our imaginations. *(Moving to the blackboard)* But wives and parents cannot know our purpose.

SCIENTIST: Which is precisely what, finest fizzler?

OPPENHEIMER: A practical weapon that releases energy in a fast, neutron chain reaction. It should be light enough to carry in an airplane.

(Hubbub and murmurs, which occur periodically throughout the scene. OPPENHEIMER uses the blackboard.)

OPPENHEIMER: Since the energy release in TNT is 3.6 x 10^{16} erg/ ton, we calculate that a one- kilogram… "magnesium" gadget should yield the equivalent of 20,000 tons of TNT.

WILSON: How much damage will it do, Oppie?

OPPENHEIMER: Depends on its efficiency and energy release, Bob. Our aim is to get as much energy…

WILSON: *(Persisting)* How much damage?

OPPENHEIMER: Severe pathological effects within 1,000 yards. *(Murmurs. A new direction)* We need to calculate cross-sections. Different configurations have different critical masses. We need to learn about "magnesium" and "copper" metallurgy. And we need to study radiation. *(Murmurs)* We don't know its effect on individuals let alone groups.

FERMI: Bob will volunteer for those experiments

(Laughter)

OPPENHEIMER: It must be small enough to transport safely. Instead of Enrico's huge slow pile, we need a small fast gadget. This chain reaction won't be controlled like his.

BETHE: How much fission fuel exists?

OPPENHEIMER: A millionth of what we need. That determines our deadline: we create the technology while Site X *(Pointing in direction of Knoxville)* enriches the "magnesium" and *(Pointing)* Hanford produces the "copper". We should have enough in twenty-four months.

BETHE: How much is enough?

OPPENHEIMER: Enough for one gadget.

FERMI: One can end the war?

OPPENHEIMER: We'll find out. We need answers to questions science never asked before. I plan weekly colloquia to stay up to date. We'll distribute notes when new recruits arrive.

FERMI: How many more do you expect?

OPPENHEIMER: One thousand five hundred.

(Responses)

OPPENHEIMER: That includes families and support personnel. If successful, our work will end the war. See you tonight on Bathtub Row. Eight o'clock for martinis. Kitty thinks we ought to celebrate my birthday.

BETHE: You don't look forty, Oppie.

OPPENHEIMER: That's because I'm thirty-nine.

(Laughter. FEYNMAN moves near FERMI to introduce himself, but FERMI strides toward OPPENHEIMER and another SCIENTIST buttonholes FEYNMAN.)

OPPENHEIMER: Have to rush off?

FERMI: Another train.

OPPENHEIMER: North to Hanford?

FERMI: East to Oak Ridge. Oppie, your people want to make a bomb. What if we poisoned German food supply with radioactive by-products instead?

(FERMI *and* OPPENHEIMER *exit together, discussing.*)

FERMI: Think about it.

FEYNMAN: (*Retrieving a package*) I respected Fermi enormously. He was a generalist, the last physicist who didn't specialize. He was equally inspired as a theorist and experimentalist. (*Noticing uncertain looks in the audience*) What's the difference? Theoretical physicists know why and how a widget works; experimental physicists make sure it does. Most of what we had to do at Los Alamos had to be done for the first time with materials that were practically unavailable. Every day I would study and read, study and read about things I didn't know much about. Weekly colloquia felt like final exams with a faculty of experts from around the world. Never before had physicists formed such a critical mass.

Scene Four:
One…and Counting

(*Crossfade to* ARLINE *in wheelchair, listening to Beethoven, "Moonlight Serenade".*)

ARLINE: Darling!

(ARLINE *sits up as* FEYNMAN *enters. Hug and kiss on the cheek.*) I could smell you coming down the hall.

FEYNMAN: My cologne or this? (*He reveals a package from behind his back.*)

ARLINE: Steak! Just what I've been craving.

FEYNMAN: No extravagance is too much for my Putsy.

ARLINE: How much?

FEYNMAN: Eight-four cents for two pounds.

(ARLINE *whistles.*)

FEYNMAN: Happy anniversary!

ARLINE: One and counting.

(ARLINE *and* FEYNMAN *blow a kiss to one another. Taking his package, she hands him hers.*)

FEYNMAN: (*He unwraps a chef's hat, apron embroidered "Bar-B-Q King," and mitt. Dons the apron first*) To protect me in the lab?

ARLINE: A perfect fit.

FEYNMAN: (*The hat*) Do I look French?

ARLINE: Oui, oui. Béarnaise sauce, please.

FEYNMAN: (*Glove*) I only get one?

ARLINE: Pretend you're playing first base.

FEYNMAN: My childhood dream. Where'd you get all this?

ARLINE: Made it.

FEYNMAN: How'd you find time?

ARLINE: Waiting for your letters.

FEYNMAN: One's in the mail?

(ARLINE *doesn't buy* FEYNMAN's *lame excuse.*)

FEYNMAN: How do I look?

ARLINE: Great. Me?

FEYNMAN: Peachy keen. Albuquerque's Presbyterian Sanitarium is treating you well. How do you feel?

ARLINE: Like an alien.

(*Responding to* FEYNMAN's *"I don't understand what you mean" look*)

ARLINE: I look out the window and pretend I've returned to the primordial Jewish home, the desert. How's the physics sanitarium?

FEYNMAN: Guess how I'm identified?

ARLINE: Boy genius.

FEYNMAN: Nope.

ARLINE: Future professor.

FEYNMAN: (*Pulling out his wallet*) My name is "Number 185". I reside at "Special List B". My signature is "not required". We're non-entities, the place isn't marked on maps, and we can't vote…

ARLINE: FDR. needs yours?

FEYNMAN: Can't get divorced…

ARLINE: I *like* it…

FEYNMAN: Can't adopt children.

ARLINE: And natural ones, Dope?

FEYNMAN: We can't probate a will.

ARLINE: If we stay here, we're immortal!

FEYNMAN: Wanna see my new toy? (*Pulls a drum from his rucksack and beats a tattoo on it*) Siphon's off nervous energy.

ARLINE: You can't find other ways? (*Responding to his drumming, whoops, and hollers of an impromptu dance*) Your neighbors like your "music"?

FEYNMAN: I amuse the cowpokes at the dude ranch.

ARLINE: And the dudettes?

FEYNMAN: Guess so.

ARLINE: When will your dorm be finished?

FEYNMAN: Next week. *(Thinking)* Can I have some powder?

ARLINE: Sure.

FEYNMAN: And hair pins?

ARLINE: Why not.

FEYNMAN: And a nightgown.

ARLINE: *(Lifting her arms or opening her robe)* How about this one?

FEYNMAN: I have a serious affliction, Putsy.

ARLINE: What's that?

FEYNMAN: Loving you forever.

(ARLINE and FEYNMAN embrace.)

ARLINE: See you next weekend.

FEYNMAN: I was assigned to the men's dorm. Just like college: two men per room. But if Arline couldn't be my roommate, I didn't want anyone, okay, so I opened the top bunk, messed up the sheets, laid out her nightgown, and threw some powder on the floor. When I got home that night, *everything* was back in order, and *nobody* was sleeping in my room. I kept this up for four nights until everybody was settled. *(Smiles)* No roommate.

Scene Five:
Numeracy

(Sounds of insects, birds, and wind: a desert night. Distant sound of something like "Blues in the Night" as FEYNMAN *speaks, and lights slowly fade to black.)*

FEYNMAN: Electrons intrigued me. I wanted to understand those little charges so their beautiful motion around the nucleus would be less mysterious.

(FEYNMAN *switches on a flashlight. There's another light, then another, yet another. At first, we see: lights on and off irregularly, jerky motions, random chaos. The lights gradually transform into order in synch with the music, a ballet of light swirling about the stage and auditorium gracefully. We perceive patterns, mystery, beauty. Then the dance of light ends as mysteriously as it began.*)

FEYNMAN: These? Ordinary flashlights.

(*As lights fade up, the dancers are seen for what they are: Los Alamos residents trying to find their way through the dark on a moonless night.*)

FEYNMAN: Los Alamos had no streetlights, so if you walked at night…. Scientists don't keep regular schedules. When you love your work, it isn't work. It's central to everyday life, every *hour* life, okay? New ideas start over coffee, or during an argument. When physicists congregate, ideas hop back and forth, up and down, in and out. You start in one direction and end in another. It's like a…chain reaction.

(*Daylight now,* FEYNMAN *enters the lab. The blackboard shows two equations added at intermission.*)

$$\frac{n_{B_{10}}}{n_U} = \frac{6 \cdot 2}{10} \Big/ \frac{93 \cdot 19}{235} = \frac{1.2}{7.6} = \frac{1}{6}$$

$$\frac{T_{\text{collapse}}}{T_{\text{expansion}}} = \frac{R_{Li}}{\Delta R} = \frac{2}{\frac{1}{4} \cdot 10} = 0.8$$

(*What follows is a duel. The weapons are chalk, erasers, and brains. The competition matters—chalk dust flying, erasers attacking—not the science, which no one in the audience or production will grasp.*)

BETHE: I've been thinking how boron bubbles could make the gadget more efficient…

FEYNMAN: (*Cutting him off*) That's crazy, Hans. Boron isn't fast enough. You're wrong.

BETHE: I'm wrong? You're crazy! It would work if…

(BETHE *circles the "U" for uranium but can barely add more before* FEYNMAN *attacks with chalk in one hand, eraser in the other.*)

FEYNMAN: You're mad, but have you considered the particle density of lithium.

(FEYNMAN *writes Li, but* BETHE *counters.*)

BETHE: That's ridiculous, but *this* might…

(BETHE *adds "Collapse" and "R" before Li, then* FEYNMAN *contributes "Expansion" and "ΔR."*)

BETHE: The radius of lithium over the change in the radius. Yes. Yes! Yes!!!

(*Both* BETHE *and* FEYNMAN *are ecstatic. They jump, hug, dance. Beat. Realization*)

BETHE: It's got nothing to do with my original problem. (*Puts chalk down*)

FEYNMAN: (*Surrendering his chalk*) Sorry Hans, I got carried away. I'm dumb that way: If the idea looks lousy, I say it looks lousy; if it looks good, I say it looks good. I forgot you're head of the Theoretical Division.

BETHE: I need to push ideas against someone to find my flaws. Und so, I want you to be a Group Leader.

FEYNMAN: I'm only twenty-five.

BETHE: You'll be youngest.

FEYNMAN: (*Curiosity weakening his reluctance*) Which group?

BETHE: Theoretical Computations.

FEYNMAN: Everyone calculates. What are *we* supposed to figure out?

BETHE: Energy release.

FEYNMAN: Starting with what?

BETHE: Hydrodynamics of implosions and explosions.

FEYNMAN: Sounds like fun.

BETHE: So…the pressure squared of 48…

(FEYNMAN *starts to multiply long-hand*)

BETHE: …is 2304.

FEYNMAN: How'd you do that?

BETHE: You don't know how to square numbers near 50?

FEYNMAN: Not in my head.

BETHE: *(Fast and totally self-assured)* Say your number is 47, which is three less than 50. Then the answer is about three hundred less than 2500, so that's 2200. And to find out exactly how much is left over, you square what's residual. So, for 47, that's three, squared is nine. Therefore, 47 squared is 2209. Got it?

(For a change, FEYNMAN *is speechless.)*

BETHE: You have to *notice* the numbers. *(He releases his booming peal of laughter.)*

FERMI: *(Striding in with a suitcase, wearing a fishing vest, joining* BETHE*'s familiar saying.)* "You have to *notice* the numbers."

FEYNMAN: *(Half to himself.)* Professor Fermi.

BETHE: *(Shaking hands, embracing.)* Enrico, wie gehts?

FERMI: Gut, sehr gut.

BETHE: Dick, you know Enrico?

FEYNMAN: No, but I've wanted… *(Shaking hands)* …it's an honor, Professor.

FERMI: Hans told me about his prodigy.

BETHE: *(Back to* FERMI*)* These calculations are very difficult. Dick here's our expert. He's a magician.

FEYNMAN: When I *notice* the numbers, I can usually tell what the answer is gonna look like, but this thing is complicated, I can't. Here's the problem, Professor Fermi, when…

FERMI: Wait! Boron, huh. *(Using blackboard)* It's going to come out like this. *(He draws on the board:)*

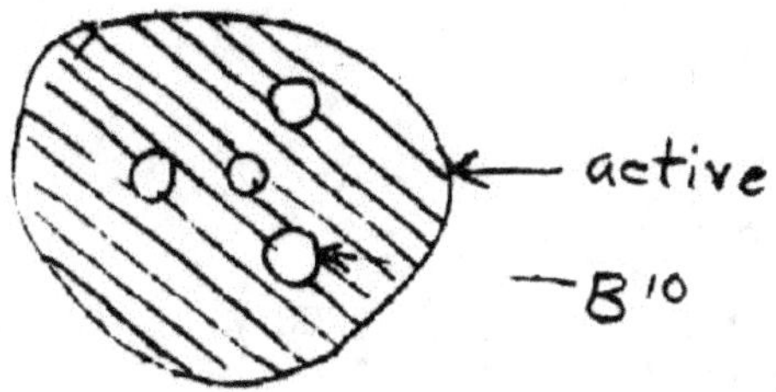

FEYNMAN: Right. *(Tail between his legs, he moves back to the blackboard to study the drawing and existing formulas.)*

FERMI: Boron has the largest absorption cross-section for fast neutrons.

FEYNMAN: You're doing my specialty ten times better.

FERMI: *(Aside)* He's your prodigy?

BETHE: Oppie recruited him personally when he recognized his brilliance. How long you stay this time?

FERMI: Consult with Oppie, then back to Chicago.

BETHE: You travel too much.

FERMI: Tell me.

BETHE: You should move here.

FERMI: Tell Laura.

BETHE: Stay and help us.

FERMI: Maybe next year.

BETHE: How's Leo?

FERMI: Baiting the brass hats more than ever.

BETHE: He's not a team player.

FERMI: Arthur dismissed him from Met Lab, temporarily. We can't discuss work or secrets with him.

BETHE: *(Still recruiting)* Laura would like the mountains.

FERMI: Yes.

BETHE: And interesting people.

FERMI: What about culture?

BETHE: Have you heard this?

(BETHE *starts "Home on the Range".* FERMI *joins in as* FEYNMAN *steps downstage.)*

FEYNMAN: When Fermi lectured, his clarity of exposition and perfection of the whole made it look obvious, beautiful. I wanted him to see me capable of numerical magic.

(Colleagues enter with mugs for coffee break, handing ones to BETHE *and* FERMI.*)*

FEYNMAN: Okay friends, or are you suckers? I hereby challenge everyone that I can solve in sixty seconds any problem you can state in ten seconds—to within ten percent accuracy? Bet a buck! Step right up.

FUCHS: You expect us to soil our brains with lowly numbers instead of symbols, abstract and pure?

OPPENHEIMER: Okay Princeton, for a dollar. What's the sum of the series $1 + (1/2)^4 + (1/3)^4 + (1/4)^4 + \ldots$

WILSON: *(Serving as timekeeper)* Go!

FEYNMAN: *(Beating rhythmically on the table to exhume the numbers)* One point zero eight.

WILSON: How accurate is that?

OPPENHEIMER: Couple of percent margin of error.

FEYNMAN: Where's my buck?

OPPENHEIMER: Double or nothing: give it to me exactly.

WILSON: Go!

FEYNMAN: *(Thinks.)* Pi to the fourth over ninety.

(Applause as OPPENHEIMER *groans. He doffs his porkpie hat, adds* FEYNMAN's *$2 winnings.)*

WILSON: Okay bongo boy, for two bucks: what's the tenth binomial coefficient in the expansion of

$(1 + x)^{20}$? Go!

FEYNMAN: *(More drumming, a different rhythm for a harder problem, then triumphant again!)* 1.8×10^5.

(More groans. WILSON *puts two dollars in* OPPENHEIMER's *hat.)*

FERMI: *(Brandishing his dollar)* For the pot, plus a buck. What's the tangent of ten to the hundredth?

WILSON: Go!

FEYNMAN: *(Again drumming. His rhythm slows, slows further. He gesticulates with his arms and legs hoping this will help him deliver the answer. It doesn't. Knock out!)* Nuts!

(Colleagues laugh as FERMI *collects his winnings from* OPPENHEIMER's *hat.)*

FERMI: Repeat after me… *(Conducting the others)* you have to *notice* the numbers.

Scene Six:
Literacy

(Crossfade to three New Mexicans conversing as something like "Hoe-Down" from Copeland's "Rodeo" is heard. They are mystified, not dim-witted.)

LOCAL MAN: *(In media res)* …and if you overhear 'em talking to a clerk, they hardly make sense for all the accents. I hear it's a home for pregnant WACs.

SECOND MAN: Nope. They're doing submarine research where no one would expect it.

LOCAL WOMAN: *(Reading her letter in local newspaper)* "To The Editor: Since I live on highway 502, I am fully aware of the stream of trucks heavily loaded on their way *up* the mesa, but empty on their way *down*. This is another New Deal boondoggle wasting taxpayer money!"

FEYNMAN: Security affected where we could go and how often. We got used to it. We could only write to relatives and friends. And we got used to that. So did they. Soon after arriving, mail censorship began. I *never* got used to that.

ARLINE: *(In her hospital bed, finishing a letter)* "Richard, the least you can do is write your family regularly. Count me in on your dad's plan. PS: I like enticing you."

(FEYNMAN shrugs, sound of ringing telephone.)

(Lights up on GROVES, stationed between the FEYNMANS.)

GROVES: Please come down.

(FEYNMAN joins GROVES.)

GROVES: Mr Feynman, what's this?

FEYNMAN: *(Examining a letter)* A letter from my father.

GROVES: Yes, *this*?

FEYNMAN: Dots around different words?

(GROVES *nods.*)

FEYNMAN: Looks like code.

GROVES: We know that. What does it say?

FEYNMAN: I don't know. *(Beat)* It's in code.

GROVES: Mr Feynman, regulation 4(e): "Codes, ciphers or any form of secret writing will not be used". *(Holding another letter)* What's *this*?

FEYNMAN: *(Brightening)* A letter from my wife!

GROVES: What is TWZ TX3Q?

FEYNMAN: That's a code too.

GROVES: What's the key to it?

FEYNMAN: I don't know. It's a game. My family writes in codes they *think* I can't decipher.

GROVES: *(Thinking this over, looks him up and down.)* They'll have to send the key inside their letters.

FEYNMAN: I don't want a key!

GROVES: *(Quickly.)* We'll take it out before you get it!

FEYNMAN: I'll inform her immediately. *(Crossing back to his lab)* "Dear Arline: It's a long story, but if you could write me differently, the censor would be a lot happier. *(As he is about to sit, telephone rings.)*

GROVES: Please come down.

(FEYNMAN *does.*)

GROVES: Regulation 8(z), Dick: "Information concerning censorship regulations or discourse on the subject is prohibited".

FEYNMAN: You said you wanted her to write different letters!

GROVES: You can't *write her* about censorship. It's against the law to censor civilian mail. Tell her in person.

FEYNMAN: Soon as I can.

(*Lights up on* ARLINE, *reading a newspaper advertisement:*)

ARLINE: "Send your boyfriend a letter on a jigsaw puzzle. We sell the blank, you write your letter, take the puzzle apart, and mail it."

(ARLINE *grins at audience. Across the stage,* GROVES *pours puzzle pieces out of a box. Long telephone ring buttons the beat.*)

FEYNMAN: (*Crossing downstage to address the audience*) See how it's easier to have fun than consider where the work is headed? It's simpler to stop thinking than to keep thinking. (*New direction*)A fence surrounded us; we wore security badges; and we lived with censorship. All to save the world from totalitarianism.

(FEYNMAN'*s chair now occupied by* KLAUS FUCHS *playing a tentative paradiddle rhythm on* FEYNMAN'*s drum.*)

FEYNMAN: You said you'd been practicing.

(FEYNMAN *and* FUCHS *laugh.*)

FEYNMAN: Klaus, you think we got too much security around here or not enough?

FUCHS: (*German accent with English inflections since England was his home after Germany.*) Why?

FEYNMAN: Seen the hole in the fence behind the Tech Area?

FUCHS: Ya, sure. Kids climbing through it for weeks.

FEYNMAN: Me too. I sneak in that way in the morning then go home by the front gate.

FUCHS: Und so?

FEYNMAN: It confuses the guards. They want to check me off for leaving but have no record that I arrived.

FUCHS: What do they say?

FEYNMAN: "You can't leave, you're not even here."

FUCHS: Und you replied?

FEYNMAN: Listen, buddy, you're giving me an existential crisis.

FUCHS: Next time, say you're a spy.

FEYNMAN: You think Groves could snoop 'em out?

FUCHS: We solve mysteries better zan ze Army.

FEYNMAN: Who would you suspect?

FUCHS: *(After a moment)* You.

FEYNMAN: Ritchie Feynman?

FUCHS: Analyze ze facts.

FEYNMAN: Such as?

FUCHS: Someone who gets letters in code.

FEYNMAN: Right.

FUCHS: Someone involved in different parts of the work.

FEYNMAN: So are others.

FUCHS: Someone free to come and go at will. *(Beat)* Visiting Arline again zis weekend?

FEYNMAN: So.

FUCHS: *(Holding out his keys)* Borrow my Buick again?

FEYNMAN: *(Taking the keys)* What about you? Klaus Fuchs...you *sound* like a Nazi.

FUCHS: If I loved Hitler, you think I would fight in ze underground, leave my family, flee to England? I think *you're a* spy!

FEYNMAN: Little Ritchie…

(*But* FUCHS *is gone in a gale of laughter. Sound of a huge explosion.* FEYNMAN *is unfazed.*)

FEYNMAN: Ordnance testing. Down in the valley.

Scene Seven:
This Land Is Your Land

(*Something like Ives's "Variations on 'America'" establishes in crossfade. A group of immigrants marches on, stops, faces center. Simultaneously, they raise their right hands and begin the oath of citizenship*)

NEW CITIZENS: I hereby declare that I renounce and abjure all allegiance and fidelity to any foreign prince, potentate, state or sovereignty…

(LAURA *breaks from the group,* FERMI *pursues her as the others quietly continue the oath behind them:*)

NEW CITIZENS: …of whom or which I have heretofore been a subject or citizen; that I will support and defend the Constitution and laws of the United States of America against all enemies, foreign and domestic; that I will bear true faith and allegiance to the same; that I will bear arms on behalf of the United States when required by the law; that I will perform noncombatant service in the Armed Forces of the United States when required by the law; that I will perform work of national importance under civilian direction when required by the law; and that I take this obligation freely without any mental reservation or purpose of evasion.")

FERMI: You will like the mountains, desert too.

(FERMI, *responding to* LAURA's *stare:*)

FERMI: We'll be together without me shuttling.

(LAURA *harrumphs.*)

FERMI: I could help with children.

(*Even louder response.*)

FERMI: You'll like Site Y.

LAURA: I love Chicago.

FERMI: You didn't want to move here.

LAURA: Then was then; now is now.

FERMI: In two years, you won't want to leave.

LAURA: You expect logical emotions? New Mexico too remote, too few people.

FERMI: They have a library, chamber music, square dances…

LAURA: Yippee!

FERMI: There's a fence around so children roam free.

LAURA: From madhouse of fascism to a desert concentration camp. We're not even Japanese.

FERMI: We return to Chicago after war.

LAURA: Promise?

FERMI: (*Raising his hand as at the beginning of the scene*) Like George Washington, I cannot tell a lie.

(FERMI *kisses* LAURA. *She raises her right hand too as they conclude the oath in synch with other new citizens.*)

EVERYONE: So help me God!

(*Jump cut to Los Alamos.* LAURA *leading the singing of "Happy Birthday" as* SCIENTISTS *enter with a birthday cake welcoming the* FERMIS *on his birthday. Singing ends in cacophony of accents and greetings in foreign languages evoking the Tower of Babel. "Many more", "Long live his eminence", "Welcome to Laura".* FERMI *blows out the candles.* OPPENHEIMER *hands him a fishing pole with a bow.*)

BETHE: A fission pole!

FERMI: Friends make it feel like home.

LAURA: *(Her perspective transformed)* It really does. Incredible vista covers limitazioni, like no…

WILSON: Paved streets.

BETHE: No traffic jams.

LAURA: *(Leading the game she unintentionally began)* No…

OPPENHEIMER: In-laws.

FEYNMAN: Nuclear families only.

LAURA: No…

FERMI: Unemployed.

OPPENHEIMER: No idle rich.

BETHE: No starving poor.

LAURA: No…

WILSON: Bathtubs.

BETHE: Showers only.

LAURA: *(Pointedly)* These showers safe.

WILSON: Summer camp for boys, year-round.

LAURA: Boys *and* girls. The hospital breaks maternity record for community this size.

OPPENHEIMER: One-fifth of married women pregnant at any given time.

BETHE: I heard Groves wants something done.

LAURA: Enforced separation?

FEYNMAN: The Army's going to pull out.

(Groans cut short by a huge explosion. For a split-second it is mistaken as the gadget. The FERMIS, *newcomers, are especially startled.)*

OPPENHEIMER: Night shots. No reason to be on edge, really. Don't go…

(But the mood has changed. OPPENHEIMER *can't keep the party alive. Guests exit quietly with flashlights.* FEYNMAN *returns to his dorm.)*

(Crossfade to SZILARD, *in Chicago, in a pinspot opposite his colleagues, reading from his memorandum. He could be off the stage, in an aisle say, to emphasize his ostracization.)*

SZILARD: 6 March 1945. Dear Mr President: Secrecy has prevented adequate contact between scientists and those responsible for policy. These weapons will adversely affect the postwar position of the United States and make urban centers vulnerable to surprise attack. International controls should be considered involving Great Britain and the Soviet Union. Our demonstration of atomic bombs will precipitate a race between the U.S. and Russia. Yours very truly, *(Signing so audience knows he's written this)* L Szilard.

*(*SZILARD *folds letter, places it into an envelope, and seals it as lights crossfade.)*

Scene Eight:
Beloved Letters

*(*ARLINE *in bed writing, frailer, listening to something like Fred Astaire singing "Let's Face the Music and Dance."* FEYNMAN *is in his Los Alamos dorm.)*

FEYNMAN: "Dearest Putsy: It snowed up here, but it's not as cold or depressing or ugly as New York. Clouds roll in across the valley and dissect the mountains. The exquisite vista stirs in me irrational, ineffable feelings. *(Beat)* Jeez, maybe I'm getting an aesthetic consciousness or something. Don't report me to any scientists. Still loving you."

ARLINE: "Dearest Coach. My engraved stationery just arrived so I'm trying it out. Hope you like it 'cause I ordered a duplicate set for you. Not 'Mrs Richard P. Feynman'. I thought you'd prefer 'Mr Arline Greenbaum'."

FEYNMAN: "Dear One. My handwriting isn't as pretty as yours, not my hands, hair, or face either, but now my stationery is. You're silly and cute and lots of fun."

ARLINE: "Darling. The blank sheet enclosed is not written in invisible ink. Nor code. Mail it back with a fresh piece of *your* stationery. I'm dying to see what friction between the sheets creates. Call it an experiment in spontaneous combustion. Or the yearning of separated spouses. Come soon. I'm light as a feather. Your Putsy, always."

FEYNMAN: "You must drink your milk and get your weight back over 100 pounds. I love only you. PS: My chest X-ray is clear."

ARLINE: "Sorry I'm moody. I'm drinking so much milk I've grown horns and started chewing a cud; udders in usual place. Darling, I think the restlessness I feel is pent up emotion. We'd both feel happier if we released our desires at last. Come soon. Dance with me."

FEYNMAN: (*Crossing the stage*) "You are beautiful. Your strength rises and falls like a mountain stream. I am a reservoir for your strength—without you, I would be empty and weak. See you Friday evening."

(*Arriving at* ARLINE's *side,* FEYNMAN *awakens her with a kiss.*)

ARLINE: The music, Coach. I've reserved a special place for you on my dance card.

(ARLINE *gets out of bed slowly.* FEYNMAN *supports her. They move to "Let's Face the Music and Dance", but she is exhausted immediately and falters.*)

ARLINE: Make love with me.

FEYNMAN: Oh, Putsy?

ARLINE: I want to; I need to.

(ARLINE *and* FEYNMAN *return to the bed, continue moving to the music, and begin to consummate their marriage at last. Beat. Huge explosion, another night test.)*

(Crossfade to Chicago. SZILARD *gleefully opening an embossed envelope.)*

SZILARD: "Dear Professor Szilard: Thank you for a copy of your memorandum to the President, which I have read with great interest. I would be happy to discuss these matters with you in my Manhattan apartment next month on May. 8. Sincerely, Eleanor Roosevelt."

(The largest explosion yet eradicates SZILARD*'s hope from this response. His elation turns to sorrow as he begins a new letter.)*

SZILARD: "Dear Mrs Roosevelt: Add my deepest condolences to those of a grieving world. Your husband served men and women of every nation who yearn for a world at peace. I look forward to rescheduling our meeting at your earliest convenience. Nothing is more important to me. With deepest condolences and profound sorrow, *(Signing so audience knows he's written this)* L Szilard."

Scene Nine:
Wins

(Crossfade to Los Alamos lab where BETHE, OPPENHEIMER, *and the* FERMIS *listen to Truman's radio broadcast announcing Nazi surrender. Shrieks of joy and cries of relief as everyone celebrates.)*

BETHE: *(Pouring champagne, then a toast more heavily accented than usual.)* To Eisenhower and all the Allied Victors! To V-E Day!

OTHERS: To V-E Day!

BETHE: I never considered myself a Jew until zat little man stripped me of my post. I was one of the first out the university door in '33. A hundred physicists followed, wandering in exile, until many of us landed here. Defeating Nazism gave us a moral purpose for living. Now we need a new one.

OPPENHEIMER: We must finish the job, Hans.

BETHE: We have, Oppie. Western civilization preserved, the enemy vanquished.

FERMI: One enemy.

BETHE: *The* enemy.

OPPENHEIMER: The Japanese have tenacity.

FERMI: Fight to final breath.

BETHE: They can't stay stubborn forever.

FERMI: Bataan?

OPPENHEIMER: Iwo Jima.

FERMI: Okinawa.

OPPENHEIMER: Kamikaze.

LAURA: *(Absorbing what she has heard.)* Enrico, what we should tell the children?

FERMI: I don't know what to say. Or think.

BETHE: *(To* OPPENHEIMER*)* You think we go ahead like before? Test gadget, then…

OPPENHEIMER: *(Eyeing* LAURA*)* I think this is not the time to discuss the future.

LAURA: I go. *(She does.)*

FERMI: Alamogordo is only an experiment.

BETHE: The largest ever attempted.

OPPENHEIMER: And an unsuccessful one if problems continue to out-pace solutions.

BETHE: And if it succeeds?

OPPENHEIMER: We report up the chain of command.

FERMI: We're depending on your calculations, Hans.

OPPENHEIMER: The test date's set.

BETHE: When?

FERMI: Eight weeks...and counting

BETHE: July.

OPPENHEIMER: Groves targeted the Fourth.

(BETHE *turns to the blackboard as lights crossfade to* FEYNMAN *in his dorm and* ARLINE *at her sanitarium. She is singing the last few bars of "Happy Birthday" as he opens her package. He reads a mock newspaper headline.*)

FEYNMAN: "Entire Nation Celebrates Birthday of Dick Feynman." (*Reading the accompanying card as Arline speaks its message.*)

ARLINE: "Happy 27, Coach. My latest mail-order extravagance. Come soon to celebrate our anniversary.

FEYNMAN: (*Whispering.*) Two years...and counting.

ARLINE: "How about Donald for a boy, Matilda for a girl?"

(*Crossfade to Chicago*)

COMPTON: Leo, I appreciate your concern about post-war policy.

SZILARD: We should not conduct a test until that's settled.

COMPTON: The test only reveals if the gadget works.

SZILARD: And where will that lead? Fear of Germany drove us. It's not clear now why we're still working.

COMPTON: *(Moving further into* SZILARD*'s light)* President Truman decides, Leo.

SZILARD: He can't grasp what we know.

COMPTON: Which is why a scientific panel will hear your concerns—and those of your colleagues.

SZILARD: Who's on it?

COMPTON: Lawrence, Fermi, Oppenheimer. *(Beat)* Me. We'll discuss if the war could end with a demonstration instead of using the gadget against a live target.

SZILARD: You know what I think.

COMPTON: Yes, but Los Alamos may not.

SZILARD: Nobody could think straight in a place like that. I'll go tell them myself.

COMPTON: Groves won't let you into New Mexico! When the scientific panel meets in June, I'll take the recommendations of you and your Met Lab colleagues. You have ten days. *(Starts to exit)*

SZILARD: Jim Franck will help.

*(*COMPTON *stops, turns back to* SZILARD*.)*

SZILARD: The other boys are confused about what a moral issue is.

Scene Ten:
Losses

(Crossfade to FEYNMAN *at* ARLINE*'s bedside. She could be fitted with oxygen to breathe.)*

FEYNMAN: Dearest Wife: I am always too slow. I understand at last how sick you are. It is a time to comfort you as you wish to be comforted, not as I think you should wish to be comforted....You will get better. I adore a great and patient woman. Forgive me for my slowness to understand. I am your husband. I love you.

(FEYNMAN *holds* ARLINE's *hand and kisses her a last time. Crossfade to Chicago.*)

SZILARD: (*Delivering a copy of the report*) The panel should pay special attention to the sections I marked.

COMPTON: (*Reading*) "These considerations make an unannounced attack against Japan inadvisable. If the United States were the first to release this destruction upon mankind, she would sacrifice public support throughout the world, precipitate the race for armaments, and prejudice the possibility of reaching an international agreement on the future control of such weapons."

SZILARD: (*Reciting from memory*) "More favorable conditions could be created if nuclear bombs were first revealed to the world by a demonstration before representatives of the United Nations."

COMPTON: "We urge that use of nuclear bombs be considered a problem of national policy rather than military expediency, and that this policy be international control of the means of nuclear warfare." The panel will consider your report, Leo.

SZILARD: (*Locking eyes*) We're sending a copy to Secretary of War Stimson too.

(*Crossfade to* FEYNMAN *in the same position and light as above.* ARLINE *and her hospital bed have disappeared.*)

BETHE: (*From a void or* FEYNMAN's *memory*) Dick, you need a vacation.

(FEYNMAN, *crossing slowly back to his dorm where lights reveal* BETHE:)

FEYNMAN: I'm fine.

BETHE: Go back to Far Rockaway. I'll get in touch when we need you.

FEYNMAN: Humans figure how to live despite knowing death will come: we laugh, we joke, we love. The difference for Arline and me was quantitative—we were married less than three years—the psychological problem was the same. We had a hell of a good time together.

(BETHE *exits in one direction,* FEYNMAN *in another. He stops and addresses the audience as a pretty dress flies in upstage.*)

FEYNMAN: I must have done something to myself mentally. I didn't cry until about a month later when I was walking past a department store and noticed a pretty dress, "Arline would like that." *Then* it hit me.

Scene Eleven:
Franck Opinions

(*Crossfade to Los Alamos lab and dim light up on* SZILARD *in Chicago. His presence shadows places that blocked his words and physical presence. He remains in half-light until he exits at Trinity.*)

FERMI: Physics has never been Leo's life.

OPPENHEIMER: He's as passionate about politics as science.

FERMI: Maybe more.

COMPTON: What if he and Jim Franck are right? A demonstration on an uninhabited island might save lives.

FERMI: And if it fizzled?

OPPENHEIMER: Even if it didn't, we'd lose the advantage of surprise.

FERMI: When will Oak Ridge have enough "magnesium" for a gadget?

OPPENHEIMER: Next month.

FERMI: Wasting it all on demonstration makes zero sense.

OPPENHEIMER: Leo's no team player. He thinks he's Cassandra.

FERMI: He's wasting time thinking about the future.

COMPTON: Wasting?

FERMI: The Chicago boys finished their assignments months ago. They don't live in the present anymore.

COMPTON: And here?

OPPENHEIMER: Total absorption in immediate tasks.

FERMI: There's no time to think.

OPPENHEIMER: The gadget will save lives.

COMPTON: You're sure?

OPPENHEIMER: Wasted hours means wasted lives. Can the gadget be worse than firebombing Tokyo?

FERMI: Eight-six thousand killed. Premiere Suzuki says his people will never surrender unconditionally.

OPPENHEIMER: An invasion would cost tens of thousands of American lives, hundreds of thousands of Japanese. We're responsible for preventing that.

COMPTON: Leo thinks we're opening the door to an era of destruction.

FERMI: Some of us feel responsible for opening the doors of science. No one stops its progress. Any fault is with those who want war not those who want knowledge. (*Wads up the Franck report and throws it in wastebasket.*) That's *my* Franck opinion.

OPPENHEIMER: Here's my recommendation: "We can propose no technical demonstration likely to bring an end to the war; we see no acceptable alternative to direct military use".

(OPPENHEIMER *signs.* FERMI *nods agreement and signs immediately. They turn to* COMPTON.)

FERMI: If the test fails, our recommendation is meaningless anyway.

COMPTON: And if it succeeds?

OPPENHEIMER: Reports up the chain of command. President Truman has a big decision to make.

(COMPTON *signs.* SZILARD *slumps, buries his head in his hands.*)

COMPTON: You think there's any stopping the momentum of two billion dollars? (*Exits*)

Scene Twelve:
All Hallowed Eve

(*Crossfade as nighttime desert comes to* FERMI *and* OPPENHEIMER. *The stage becomes more open and spacious than before by adding a star drop or flying out walls. Winds, distant thunderstorms, and lighting put everyone on edge.* SZILARD, *still seen faintly in Chicago, is composing another document.* BETHE *and* WILSON *join* FERMI *and* OPPENHEIMER.)

FERMI: Why name the test Trinity, Oppie?

BETHE: A holy experiment that reveals a mystery?

WILSON: Death followed by resurrection?

OPPENHEIMER: Something like that.

WILSON: Should a chaplain attend?

(Dead silence)

OPPENHEIMER: Relax. Teller says the chance of igniting the atmosphere is one in three million.

BETHE: Edward's calculations put me at such ease.

WILSON: *(Staring out)* What's this place called?

OPPENHEIMER: McDonald's.

BETHE: Farm?

OPPENHEIMER: Ranch.

FERMI: How far from Los Alamos?

OPPENHEIMER: Two hundred miles south.

WILSON: *(Looking afar)* What's over there?

OPPENHEIMER: Jornada del Muerto.

BETHE: Meaning?

FERMI: Journey of the dead.

WILSON: This wind could lift debris and shower the region with radioactive dust. Maybe we should postpone.

OPPENHEIMER: The weather must change!

(Loud crack of lightning and thunder. Other SCIENTISTS enter, including SEDs.)

BETHE: What if it fails?

OPPENHEIMER: Bainbridge climbs the tower to check.

FERMI: Another PhD serving science. *(Beat)* Let's guess the blast size. I've got a little test in mind. We'll have a betting pool. Oppie, collect everyone's dollar, any number between a hundred and…twenty thousand in equivalent tons of TNT. Gentlemen, place your bets.

(Each SCIENTIST *puts a dollar into* OPPENHEIMER'S *hat while announcing a number. Another presentational litany, round robin, with actors assuming new personae as needed.)*

BETHE: Eight thousand.

WILSON: One thousand, four hundred.

OPPENHEIMER: Three hundred.

SCIENTIST: Forty-five thousand.

FERMI: Edward, it's only supposed to yield twenty thousand!

SCIENTIST: I'm an optimist!

SCIENTIST: I'm not. Zero.

(Whistles all around)

OPPENHEIMER: Such confidence, Norman.

SCIENTIST: Two hundred.

FERMI: Isador?

SCIENTIST: Eighteen thousand for me.

FERMI: *(Looking around)* Where's Dick?

OPPENHEIMER: Far Rockaway. Recovering from Arline.

BETHE: Dick depressed is more cheerful than most of us exuberant.

WILSON: Think he'll make it back in time?

BETHE: I sent him a telegram, "baby expected any day".

WILSON: Hans! What's that going to make him think?

FERMI: Get his bet when he arrives. I say ten thousand.

(As group breaks up, FERMI *whispers to* BETHE.*)*

FERMI: Side bet on whether we incinerate New Mexico?

*(*COMPTON *and* GROVES *enter upstage, confer with* OPPENHEIMER, *and gaze at the sky as if to alter the threatening weather. Sounds of wind, lighting, and thunder*

are overtaken by a celestial harp— "Waltz of the Flowers".
Puzzled, the SCIENTISTS *look to one another.)*

FERMI: Tchaikovsky?

OPPENHEIMER: *The Nutcracker?*

COMPTON: In July?

GROVES: Must be radio interference.

(GROVES *crosses down center as the* SCIENTISTS *break into
groups of two and three.* GROVES *cranks his field telephone.)*

GROVES: Governor Dempsey? General Groves here.
Sorry to wake you in the middle of the night. Monday,
16 July 1945. *(Listens)*

(WILSON *pours lotion from a bottle, then passes it around.
He assumes a kneeling posture.)*

WILSON: Teller says it will protect against sunburn.

BETHE: Sunbathing in the middle of the night in the
middle of nowhere.

(A similar bottle is shared among OPPENHEIMER, GROVES,
and FERMI. *Everyone applies it under the following speech
as* SCIENTISTS *don goggles dark as welders'.)*

GROVES: *(Continuing from above)* No, I can't say where
I am. Listen closely now. You might have to declare
martial law for the state later today. *(Listens)* No, I can't
say why. I wanted to prepare you just in case. *(Listens)*
That's right, martial law. Go back to sleep now.
(Disengages his phone)

(Only GROVES *follows instructions precisely and
immediately.)*

OFFICIAL: *(Voice-over. Affect-less)* At a long siren, two
minutes to zero, all personnel whose duties do not
require otherwise will lie prone, heads away from
Ground Zero. Do not, repeat, do not face Ground Zero.

(One or two Scientists *lie down, facing upstage. Others follow.)*

Official: *(VO)* Face and eyes directed toward the ground.

(Some turn over.)

Bethe: Watch out for snakes!

Official: *(VO)* At Zero, do not watch flash directly. Turn over after it has occurred and watch the cloud.

(Some men play with their dark glasses and realize the difficulty of seeing one another.)

Official: *(VO)* Stay on the ground until the blast wave passes. At two short whistles, indicating the hazard from light and blast has passed, all personnel prepare to leave.

Wilson: Assuming the chain reaction stops.

Official: *(VO)* Remember, injury by ultraviolet light is avoided with long trousers and long sleeves.

(One Scientist *rolls down his sleeves. Another pulls socks over his cuffs. Everyone is prone except* Fermi *who will drop slips of paper to measure the blast approximately. All wear dark glasses. Beat. Loud siren)*

Wilson: I am determined to look the devil in the eye.

*(*Wilson *pivots on his stomach like a beached whale. Others follow his lead, determined to see what they have created by facing the blast downstage, the "wrong" way. One covers his mouth, another his ears, a third his eyes.* Szilard *exits Chicago wearily across the entire stage, threading his way past prone scientists. He does not see them; they do not see him. "Waltz of the Flowers" fades away as eerily as it arrived. The stage is silent for the only time in the scene.)*

*(*Feynman *rushes on, separate from everyone else, toys with dark glasses, decides not to use them. After an all but interminable silence—ten seconds?—darkness gives way*

to a primordial explosion of light and the sensation of heat that moves inexorably from the audience to the stage before disappearing into the ether. This holds as long as psychically possible. Each scientist expresses his or her amazement in a tableau including wonder, fear, loathing, piety, patriotism, ambition rewarded, prayer fulfilled—or denied—and so on.)

(As the Second Movement of Schubert's "String Quartet #14" [Death and the Maiden] begins, SCIENTISTS rise slowly, staring over the the audience at what each helped create. As the blast ebbs, pre-dawn inkiness returns. The final litany is presentational, ceremonial, measured. Actors assume as many personae and accents as necessary. Each exits deliberately after his or her final line.)

SCIENTIST: Who would have thought it would be so beautiful.

SCIENTIST: Like the halo in a medieval painting of Christ's ascension.

SCIENTIST: Bright as the light to be seen at the end of the world—and at its beginning too. Light that preceded the word that preceded the god who now seems dead.

GROVES: I no longer consider the Pentagon a safe shelter. *(Tapping the place on his uniform that denotes his expected promotion to major general.)* Brighter than two stars!

SCIENTIST: It blasted; it pounced; it bored its way right through you. It was a vision that was seen with more than the eye.

FERMI: A very intense flash of light and a sensation of heat on the parts of my body that were exposed…the countryside became brighter than in full daylight.

SCIENTIST: Prospero ignored the affairs of state for his love of books and magic…

SCIENTIST: Prometheus condemned to perpetual torture for giving the fire of the gods to humanity.

SCIENTIST: Epimetheus ignored the consequences of his own actions and those of his beloved wife, Pandora.

WILSON: In the last millisecond of the earth's existence, the last man will see what we have just seen. It's a terrible thing we made.

OPPENHEIMER: Now I am become Death, the destroyer of worlds.

Epilogue:
The Prize?

(As the Schubert fades out, WILSON *crosses to* FEYNMAN *and returns the formal coat and top hat they had exchanged in the Prologue.* FEYNMAN *dons the coat but carries the hat, now collapsed into a disk. Lighting returns us to* FEYNMAN's *Nobel ceremony. His memories are over. He's back where we met him, but the audience is not. Now it knows what he knows.)*

FEYNMAN: Monday-morning quarterback is the easiest position on any team to play. It has led me to question von Neumann's idea that "You don't have to be responsible for the entire world that you are in".

When you're doing science, you enter a different world, okay? You're using what you know to imagine what you don't know. You look at possibilities and filter some of 'em out. The wrong ones, the ugly ones, but not at first—this is very interesting—not the impossible ones. Solving a problem is a beautiful experience. Like all beauty, it gives pleasure. Original theory is absolutely beautiful because it is unsullied by experimental proofs, only as finite as your imagination's ability to grasp a possibility, a possibility of possibilities. In the ether of pure science, for finite moments—unexpected and exquisitely profound—a scientist can discover truth.

We were children, then students, grad students, teaching assistants, fellows, docs, post-docs, and full-fledged scientists. But not necessarily adults. Rabi called physicists Peter Pans of the human race: They never grow up; they always stay curious. Trinity "succeeded" twenty-eight months after I arrived at Los Alamos, and I was the first Group Leader to leave. I spent less than three years of my life solving problems with J Robert Oppenheimer.

What happened to me, what happened to the rest of us, is we started for a good reason, then you're working very hard to accomplish something and it's a pleasure, it's excitement. And you stop thinking, you know. You just stop thinking. Leo Szilard was one of the few who kept thinking, and he was ostracized for it.

When I was young, when I was single, I thought science would make good things for everybody. It was obviously useful; it was good; it was fun. After the war, I worried about the bomb. I didn't know what the future was going to look like, and I certainly wasn't sure we would last until now. Therefore, one question was this: Is there some evil involved in science? Put another way: What is the value of the science I had dedicated myself to, the thing I loved, when I saw it could do such terrible things. *(More intimate with the audience than ever before)* Have you ever done something wrong in your life? And you didn't realize it 'til afterwards? *(Taking in whatever nods or responses the audience offers)* Well, worse that being wrong is the belated awareness than you didn't even bother to consider the possibility you might be wrong.

(The Schubert returns, with the final measures of the second movement, backtimed so it ends just as FEYNMAN *and the Stockholm chandelier disappear below.)*

FEYNMAN: Atomic bombers and their bomb—our bomb, my bomb—ended the war. Peace came to the world around me. And to the world within me—head, heart, conscience, consciousness? Yes. And no. (*He puts on the top hat.*) Is Mr Feynman joking? I wish I were.

(FEYNMAN *exits slowly upstage, beneath the Stockholm chandelier, which fades away. Darkness again envelops him.*)

END OF PLAY